Junior NKIERE MAKOLONI

COMPUTER COURSES YEAR THREE SA

Junior NKIERE MAKOLONI

COMPUTER COURSES YEAR THREE SA

SciencíaScripts

Imprint
Any brand names and product names mentioned in this book are subject to trademark, brand or patent protection and are trademarks or registered trademarks of their respective holders. The use of brand names, product names, common names, trade names, product descriptions etc. even without a particular marking in this work is in no way to be construed to mean that such names may be regarded as unrestricted in respect of trademark and brand protection legislation and could thus be used by anyone.

Cover image: www.ingimage.com

This book is a translation from the original published under ISBN 978-620-6-71713-3.

Publisher:
Sciencia Scripts
is a trademark of
Dodo Books Indian Ocean Ltd. and OmniScriptum S.R.L publishing group

120 High Road, East Finchley, London, N2 9ED, United Kingdom
Str. Armeneasca 28/1, office 1, Chisinau MD-2012, Republic of Moldova, Europe
Managing Directors: Ieva Konstantinova, Victoria Ursu
info@omniscriptum.com

Printed at: see last page
ISBN: 978-620-8-51165-4

Contents

PREFACE

In recent years, the world has undergone rapid change as a result of the use and perfection of new information and communication technologies, which can now be seen in almost every area of life. Computers are currently used in companies as part of information and production system.

As defined in the Larousse dictionary, computing is the science of rational and automatic information processing; computing is considered to be a medium of knowledge in different fields of science. IT is currently used for control, surveillance, communication and many other applications that we will never be able to list in full, just to show how wide its field application is.

IT is not a miracle cure for all the ills of business; however, when used rationally within the framework of a pre-established organisation with the partners concerned, it can be a tool for development. To achieve this, it is first necessary to provide training for our students who wish to pursue their professional careers in public administration, by writing appropriate books that will enable them to study well and acquire basic knowledge of computer science. This is the very aim of this book on computer science for students in the third year of humanities, secretarial-administration option.

Although NICTs are much more widely used in companies, schools and other educational institutions are showing a very low take-up rate.

need in the use of this tool and more particularly a technical school.

We would like to thank the Ministere Provincial de l'EPST Haut-Uele and the Inspection Principale Provinciale de Haut-Uele 2 for their involvement in the production of this book, which will be of use not only to the Province of Haut-Uele but also to all the schools in our country that offer the Secretariat-Administration option.

SUMMARY

This theoretical and practical work, which is easy to understand for students in the 3eme des humanites, option Secretariat-Administration, will also serve as a compendium for teachers wishing to learn computer science, as it conforms to the national programme of Primary, Secondary and Technical Education of the Democratic Republic of Congo.

In this book we have focused on concepts such as :carrying out procedures for processing files in a folder using MS Word and hyperlinks ,analysing information and writing reports using MS PowerPoint, analysing documents and proposing solutions by creating graphs ,organising the work to be done on a daily basis using MS Outlook, planning travel and holidays using MS Outlook, presenting work a meeting using PowerPoint animations , a good command of the operation and use of the scanner, a good command of the basics of computer networks, teaching students the types of data back-up on a medium, a good command of sorting data according ascending order of fixed criteria and at the end of all these points, teaching them how to filter data using the simple and personal method.

If you follow the teaching of this book through to the end, you'll be well on the way to a successful sixth year in the humanities, and you'll no longer have any problems following up the concepts covered in the fourth year of the humanities.

We look forward to receiving your comments, criticisms and any suggestions you may have for improving this book, and we encourage every school to buy a copy. By purchasing a copy, you are encouraging scientific research.

Our thanks go entirely to Jesus Christ, who has given us success over sin.

OBJECTIVE

GENERAL OBJECTIVE

By the end of the third year of Humanites Secretariat administration, all learners will be able to use IT tools.

SPECIFIC OBJECTIVES

At the end of the school year, any third-year humanities secretariat-administration learner who has followed this course assiduously will be able to:

Carry out the procedures for processing files in a folder ;
Analysing the information and writing the report;
Analyse documents and propose solutions;
Hierarchise the work to be carried out on a daily basis;
Planning travel and time off;
Presenting the work at a meeting;
Master the operation and use of the scanner;
Mastering network concepts;
Learn more about word processing ;
Saving data on a medium ;
Sort data by ascending order of fixed criteria;
Filtering data using the simple and personalised method.

CHAPTER I

WORD INSERTION MENU

I.1. HEADER AND FOOTER

Headers and footers are areas that appear at the top and bottom of each page in a document. They are used to provide additional information and to personalise the document. The elements that can be inserted in these spaces are the page number, the date, a company logo, the title of the document, the name of the file or the name of the author, etc.

1. Go to **Insert>** **Header** or **Footer**.
2. Choose the header style you wish to use.
3. Add or modify text for the header or footer.
4. To remove a header, such as deleting it from the title page, select it, then tick the **Different first page** box.
5. Select **Close header and footer** or press Esc to exit.

To delete, select **Insert>** **Header** (or **Footer**) > **Delete header** (or **Delete footer**).

1.2. PAGE NUMBER

In the header, in the footer, in the margins or even anywhere in your document, number the pages by choosing from different styles, sober and effective or more fanciful.

1. To add page numbers, click on the **Insert** tab, then on **Page number**, in the *Heading and footer* category.
2. Choose the location where the page number should be displayed:

- **Top of page**, i.e. in the header;
- **Footer**, i.e. in the footer;
- **Page margins**, left or right ;
- **Current position**, i.e. in your document, where the cursor is, including in the header or footer to create a custom numbering, or in a rectangular text box (**Insert > Text box**) or in a more fanciful shape (**Insert > Shapes**).

3. Also specify the numbering style: **normal number**, or **with shapes** (circle, square, arrow), etc.
4. Some header/footer styles offer three views: left, centre or right of the page. In the styles reserved for margins, the choice concerns the left or right margin.

- You can also manage this alignment manually. For example, when you're editing a footer, press the **Tab** key twice to right-align the next text you type, or the page number you insert via **Page number > Current position > Normal number**.
- When you insert the page number, or when you double-click in the header or footer area, a contextual **header and footer** tab appears in blue to the right of the others. The ribbon then gives you new options for customising the top and bottom areas of the page, with a **Close** button for returning to the body

text.

- On the left of this ribbon, under the **Header and footer** tab, click **Page number > Page number format** to access certain options.

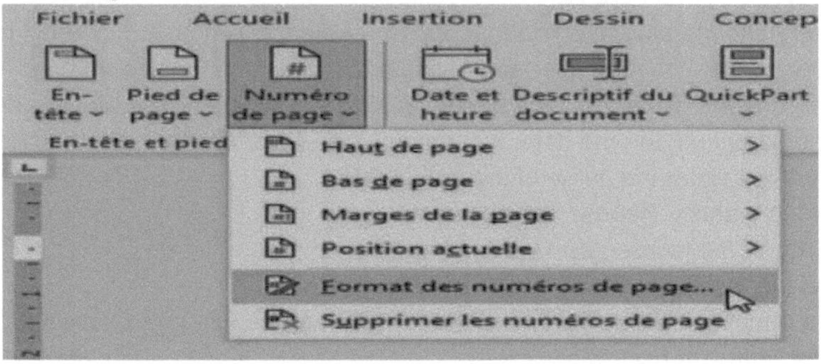

- Here you can specify the numbering format (Arabic numerals, Roman numerals, letters), the number of the first page, etc. We'll look at all these options in the other sections of this practical guide.

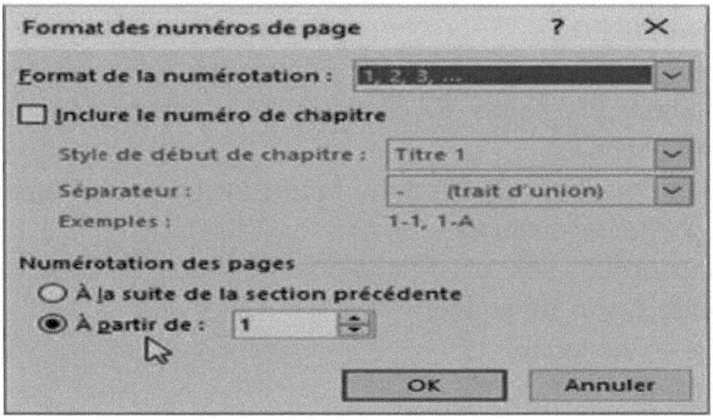

I.3.TABLE

Here's how to create an initially symmetrical array.

1. Click in the document where you want to create a table.

FIRST METHOD :

On the **Insert** ribbon, click **Table** then drag the mouse pointer to select the required number of rows and columns.

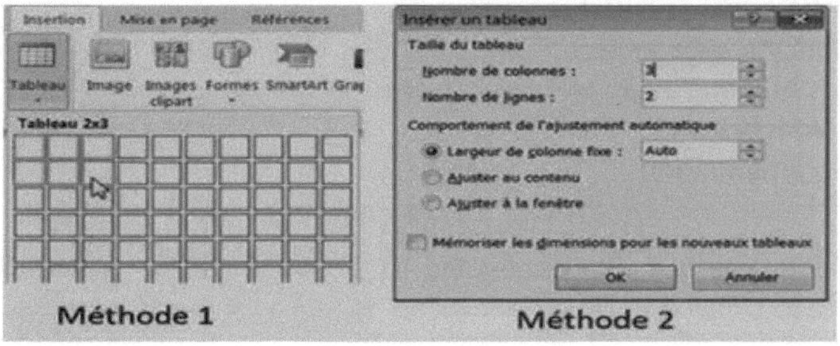

SECOND METHOD

On the **Insert** ribbon, click **Table**, **Insert Table**, then enter the appropriate values in **the Insert Table** dialog box.

1.4. TEXT ZONE

A text box is a **graphical interface element used enter or display text**. A text box can be added to a document or web page to draw attention to a specific piece of text or to move text around the file. You can format and position a text box by using the commands in the Format contextual tab or by dragging the text box with the pointer.

To insert a text box, follow these steps

1. Go to Insert > text zone.
2. Select one of the pre-formatted text boxes in the list, select Other text boxes in Office.com or select Draw a text box.
3. If you select Draw a text box, click in the document, then drag to draw the text box the size you want.
4. Enter your text.
5. Change the layout of your text.

1.5. LETTRINE

A letterhead is a decorative element generally used in documents at the beginning of a section or chapter. It consists of a large **capital letter** at the beginning of a paragraph or block of text which is two or more lines deep in normal text.

Here's how to add a letterhead;

1. Select the first character of a paragraph ;
2. Go to **Insert** then Letter ;
3. Select lettering option of your choice.

To create a letter that fits inside your paragraph, select **rejected**. To create a letterhead in the margin, outside your paragraph, select in the margin.

NB: You can change the size and font of the lettering, as well as its distance from the text.

To do this, select **lettrine>** lettrine **options**, then, under **options**, make the desired selections.

DELETING A LETTERHEAD

1. Highlight the large letter;
2. Go to insert then letter, and select **none.**

I.6. EQUATIONS

Inserting an equation

Click on the arrow below the big "*Equations* button: you can then simply select an equation. You can also display the Autres équations sur Office.com. You will not be redirected to Office.com on your browser, it's just a list that is added, with even more equations:

If none of the equations in these two lists suits you, you can click on

π Insérer une nouvelle équation at the bottom of the list.

To get an average level in mathematics and test the equations, I suggest a formula that is not very complex: the quadratic formula, the root a second-degree equation ax2+bx+c=0ax2+bx+c=0 when b2+4ac>0b2+4ac>0 :

$$x = \frac{-b \pm \sqrt{b^2-4ac}}{2a}$$

When you clicked on the equation, a new tab appeared: "*[Equation tools] Design*". It's a ritual in this course to introduce the tabs, so we'll do that here.

EQUATION OR DESIGN TOOLS

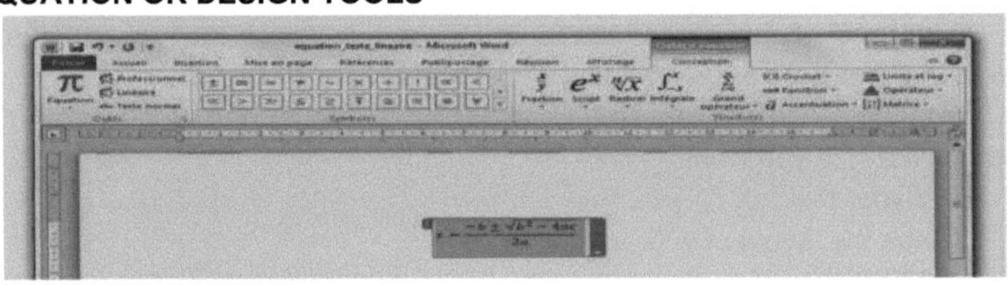

There are only three groups;

Tools

The first group is used insert a new equation at the selected location. For example, if you have selected the numerator and then click on insert equation, this new equation will become the numerator of the complete equation.

Here's an example:

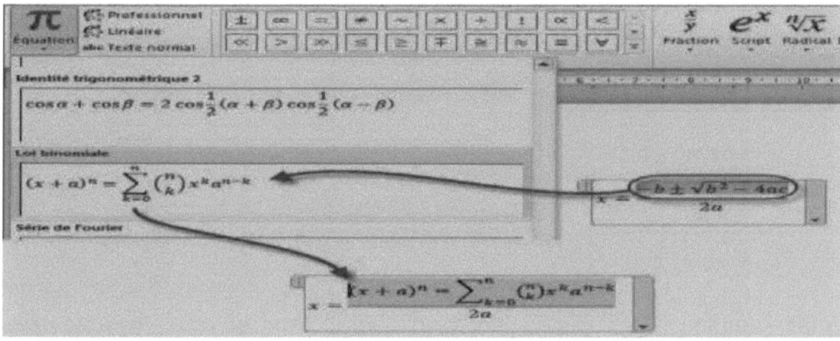

The other two functions put equations on two and one line respectively (the '/' is used as a symbol for the fraction). The third function converts the equation into normal text and vice versa.

Recapitulating with small trials, 9a gives :

- **Professional**: default functionality for the normal display of equations - as we saw in the first test document;
- **Linear**: function that displays equations on a line:
- **Text**: feature that displays equations as text. This is not the most suitable but can be useful:

$$x = (-b \pm \sqrt{}(b\char`^2 - 4ac))/2a$$

- **Linear text**: you can combine the two functions. Click on "*Text*" and on "*Linear*":

$$x=\frac{-b\pm\sqrt{b^2-4ac}}{2a}$$

$$x=\frac{-b\pm\sqrt{b^2-4ac}}{2a}$$

NB: when you want to change the way the function is displayed, remember to select the whole formula. It must be completely highlighted. To do this, use the shortcut Ctrl + A .

For your information, when formatting equations, Word uses Cambria italic as the default font, with a slightly different alignment: if a line only contains an equation with no text, it is centred; as soon as you add even one space on this same line, it takes on the alignment of the text and switches to line mode.

I.7.SYMBOLS

Inserting symbols

Click on the "*Symbols*" button and a small menu will appear:

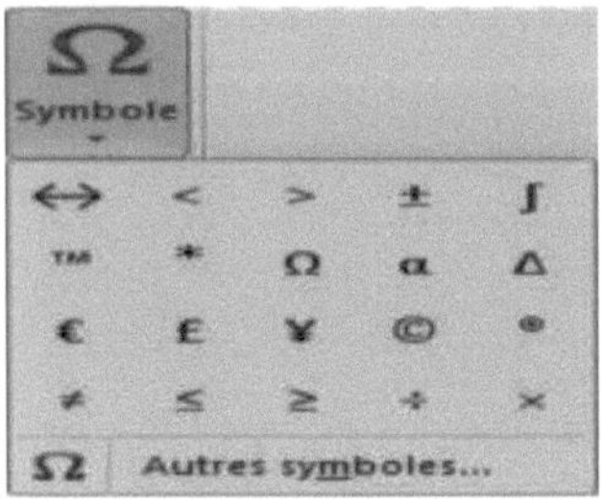

A small sample of symbols is then displayed in front of you. You can select one of them, and it will automatically appear in your document at your cursor position. You can also select Others> m(boles) to land on this window:

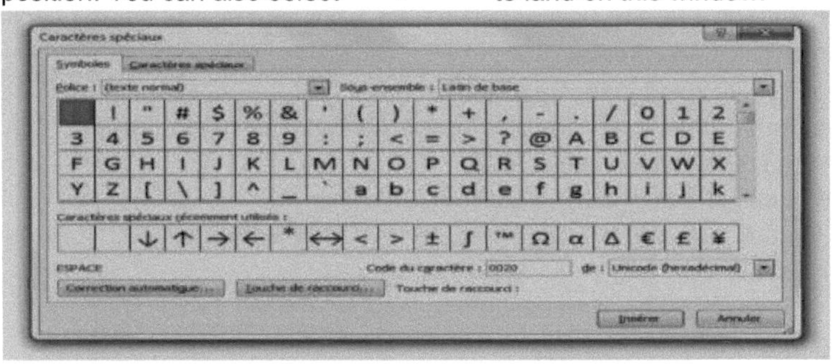

From there, a long list of characters is at your disposal.
All categories (*Basic Latin*, *Supplement Latin-1*, *Extended Latin A/B*, etc.) taken together, you can insert the symbol you want, in the font you want.
Note that recently used characters are easier to access.
Here, as in the quick menu, click on the character you want and then on "*Insert*. The character is inserted into the document, but the window remains open to allow you add other symbols.
As far as the '*Special characters*', '*Auto-correction*and '*Shortcut keys*are concerned, the first two will be covered in a chapter in the last part, while the third was covered in a chapter in the first part.

List icons

The other use for symbols here is for smart lists.

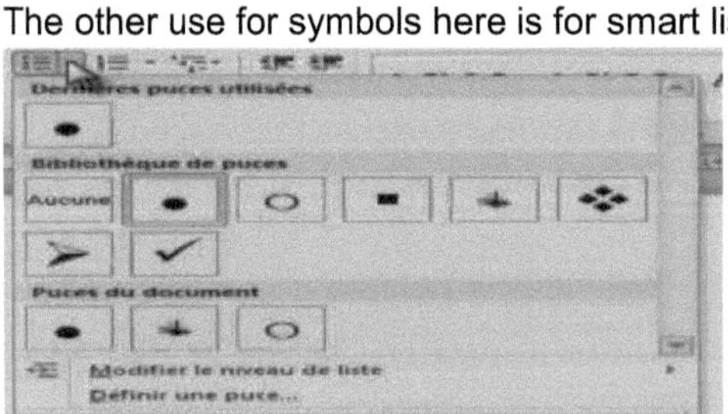

When we looked at bulleted lists, we saw that it was possible to use a symbol as a bullet, by clicking on "*Define a bullet...*" and then on "*Symbol*":

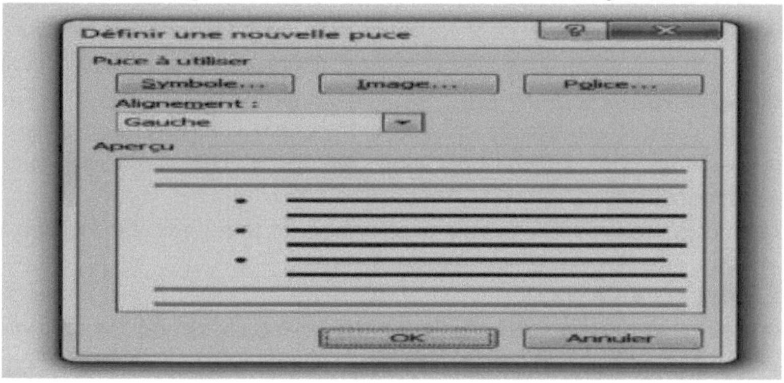

CHAPTER II

HYPERTEXT LINKS

A Hypertext Link quick access to information stored in another file, another document, a web page, an e-mail message, an image or to a specific location in your document.

Note that Word automatically creates a hypertext link when you press the Enter key or the space bar after typing a URL address such ; www.microsoft.com

You can also create a link to text or an image, or to a particular location in a document.

11.1. LINK TO A LAYOUT

PowerPoint has a 'Hyperlinkfeature that makes it easy to add links anywhere in your presentation. Adding links can make your presentation more informative, for example by including a hyperlink to a website or by providing alternatives, for example when you link to another presentation slide.

1) Open the PowerPoint presentation you wish to modify or create a new presentation.

2) Click a text box on the slide for which you want to add a link. Select the text or object to which you want your link to be connected.

3) Click on the "Insert" tab and in the "Links" group, select **Action**

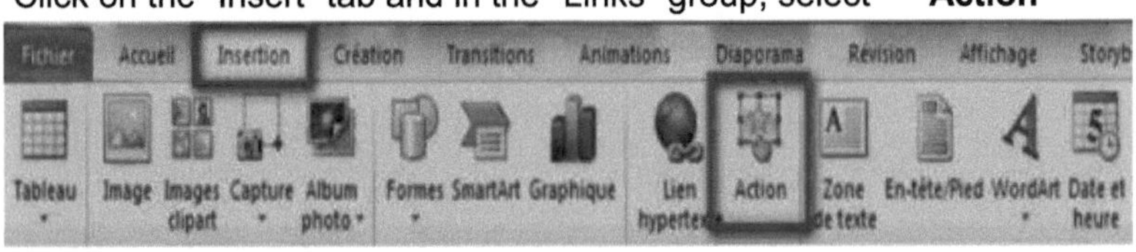

4) In the "Action settings" dialog box, select **Create a hypertext link to:** and select the down arrow to display the different options:

- Next slide
- Previous slide
- First slide
- Last slide
- Previous slide
- Slide...

. URL...

- Other PowerPoint presentation
- Other file

In this example, select **Slide** to select a specific slide title.

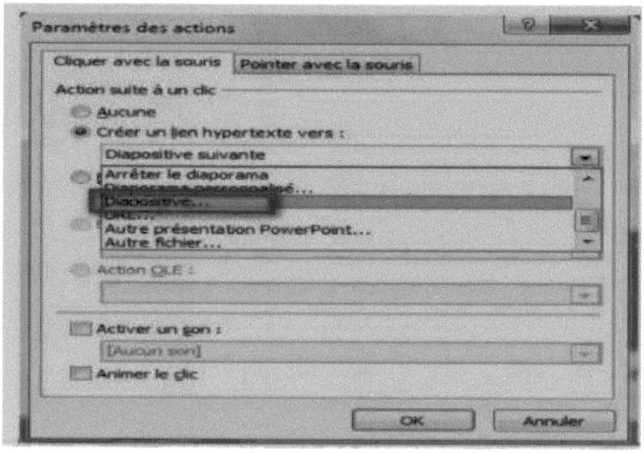

5) In the **Hypertext link to slide** dialogue box, under the slide title, choose the title of the slide to which the text will be linked. Click OK when you have made your choice.

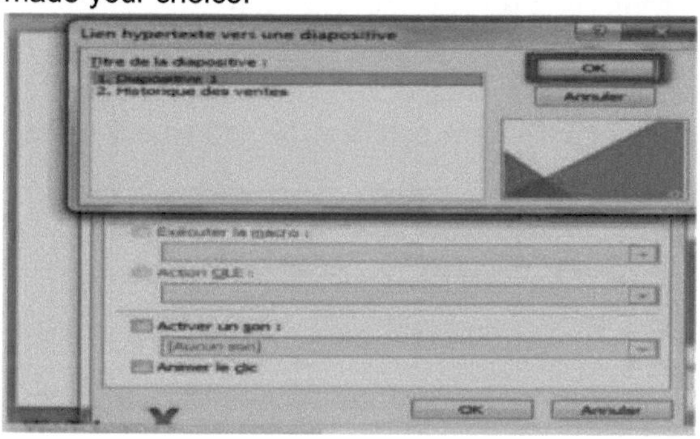

6) Click on "OK" to close the "Settings" dialog box.
of action".

11.2. LINK TO A FILE

Select text or image to use as a link.

TWO POSSIBLE METHODS FOR CREATING A LINK :

1. Right-click on it
2. Click on Hypertext link in the context menu
3. Click on the Insert tab
4. Click on Hypertext link

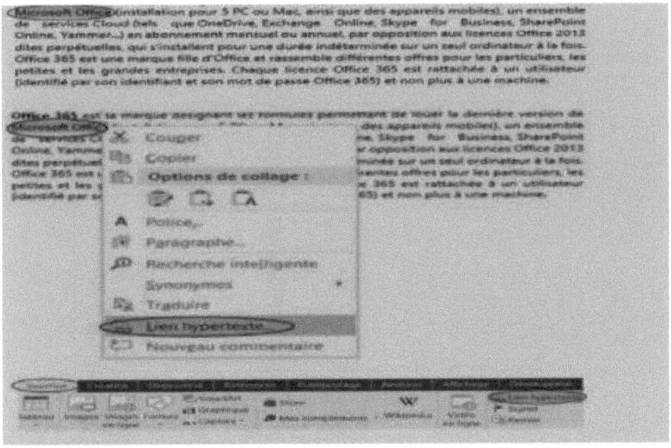

In the Insert a hypertext link dialog box, do the following
one of the following operations:

1. **CREATE A LINK TO AN EXISTING WEB PAGE OR FILE**

- Click on Existing file or web page
- Type a URL in the Address field
- If you don't know the address of a file, click on the arrow in the Look in list, then go to the file you want.

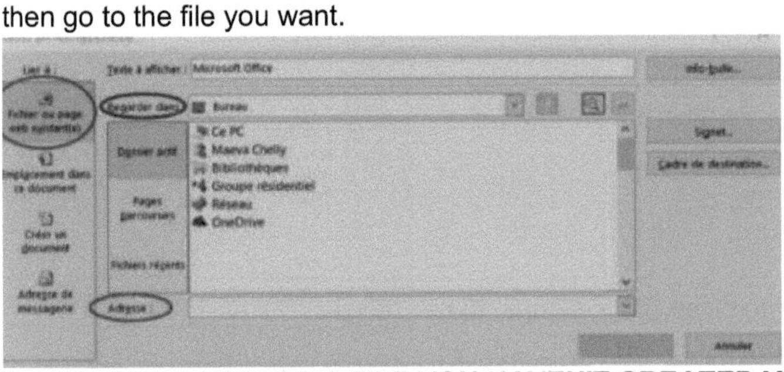

2. **CREATE A LINK TO A FILE YOU HAVEN'T CREATED YET**

- Click on Create a document
- Type the name of the new file in the New document name box
- In the When to change
- Click on Modify new document later or Modify new document now

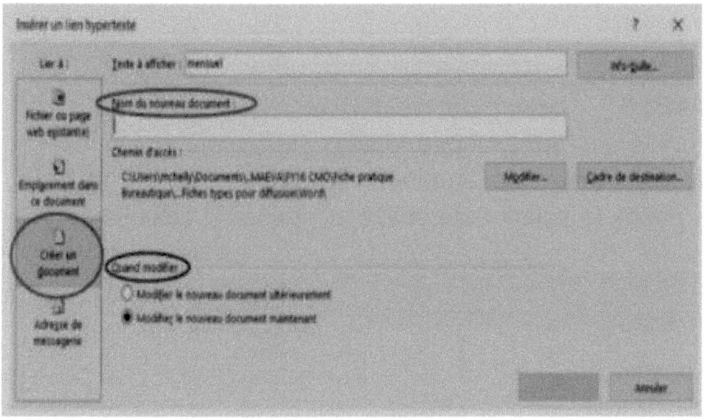
Insérer un lien hypertexte
Lier à :
Texte à afficher :
Info-bulle...
Nom du nouveau document :
Chemin d'accès :
Modifier...
Cadre de destination...
Fichier ou page web existant(e)
Emplacement dans ce document
Créer un document
Adresse de messagerie
Quand modifier :
Modifier le nouveau document ultérieurement
Modifier le nouveau document maintenant
Annuler

CHAPTER III

POWERPOINT TABLE

III.1.INSERTING A TABLE

To insert a table in PowerPoint, follow these steps ;

1. In the Ribbon, select the **Insert** tab and then click on the **Table** icon. Using your mouse, use the matrix to select the number of rows and columns in your table.

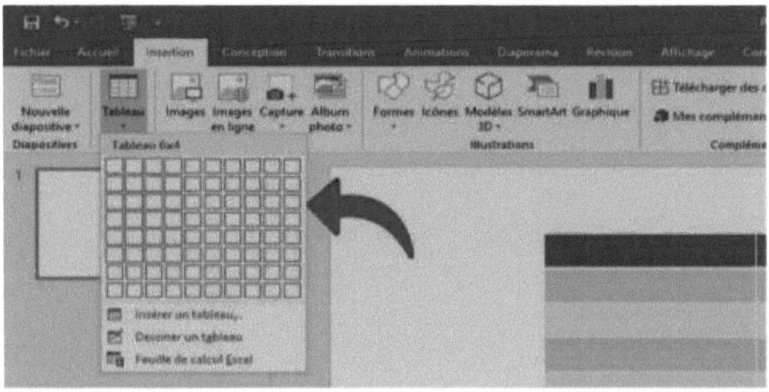

2. A new table object is then inserted into your slide. It does not all that's left to do is complete it.

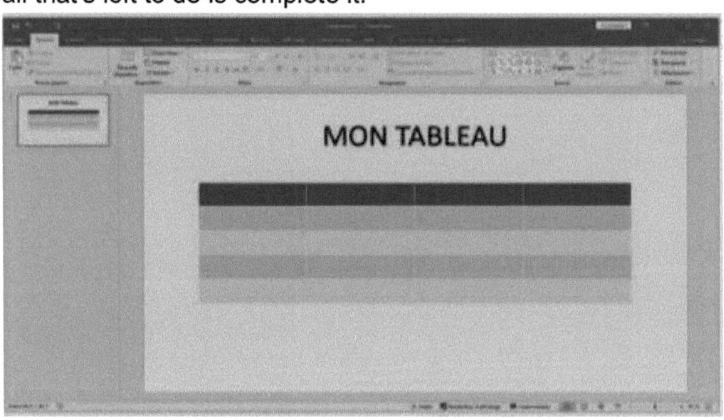

III.2.MODIFYING A TABLE

ADD A LINE

1. Click on a table cell in the row above or below which you want the new row to appear.

2. On the **Layout** tab, in the **Rows & Columns** group, perform one of the following operations:

- To add a line above the selected cell, click **Insert above**.
- To add a line below the selected cell, click **Insert at** .

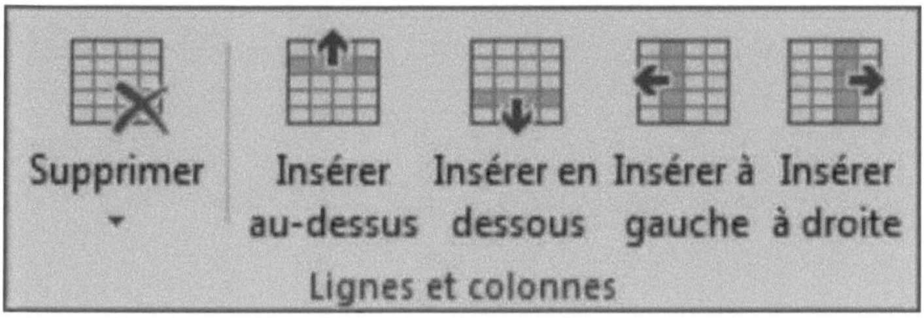

Note:

To add several rows at once, use the mouse to drag to select an equal number of rows up to the quantity you wish to add, then click **Insert above** or **Insert below**.

For example, select three existing lines, click **Insert above** or **Insert below**, and three extra lines will be added.

▪ To add a row to the end of a table, click in the rightmost cell of the last row, then press Tab.

ADD A COLUMN

1. Click on a table cell to the right or left of the column in which you want the new column to appear.
2. On the **Layout** tab, in the **Rows & Columns** group, do one of the following:

o To add a column to the left of the selected cell, click **Insert left**.

o To add a column to the right of the selected cell, click **Insert right**.

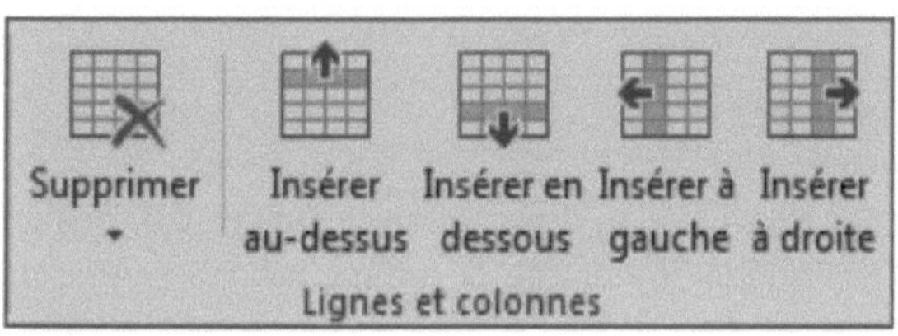

Note:

To add more than one column at a time, using the mouse, drag to select an equal number of columns up to the amount you wish to add, then click **Insert Left** or **Insert Right**. For example, select three existing columns, click **Insert Left** or **Insert Right**, and three more columns will be added.

DELETE A ROW OR COLUMN

1. Click on a table cell in the column or row to be deleted.
2. On the **Layout** tab, in the **Rows & Columns** group, click **Delete**, then click **Delete columns** or **Delete rows**.

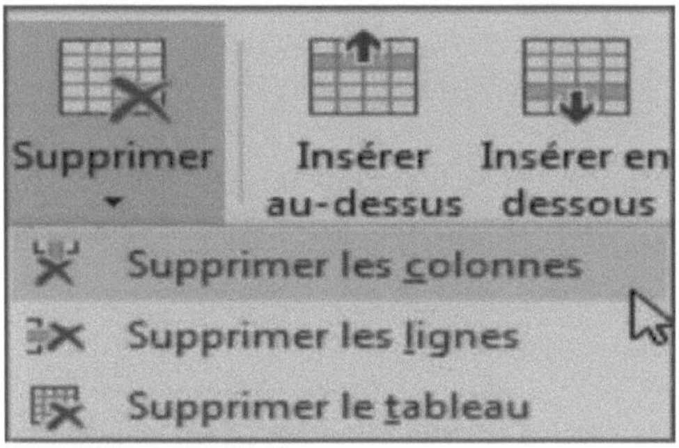

DELETE A TABLE

1. Click on the table to select it.
2. On the **Layout** tab, in the **Rows & Columns** group, click **Delete**, then click **Delete table** or press Delete on your keyboard.

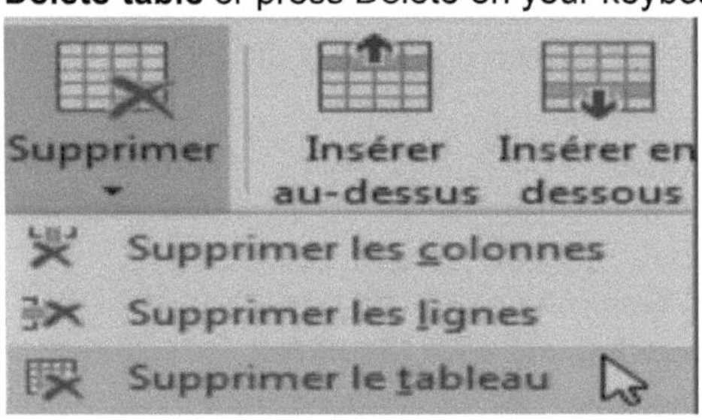

III.3.RESIZING A TABLE

To resize a table, follow these steps :

1. Click on the table to be resized.
2. On the table border, point to a sizing handle, then when the pointer becomes a -, click and drag the handle to enlarge or reduce the table. A sizing handle is the cluster of dots that appears at the corners and sides of the table.

Please note the following points:

4- To maintain the same ratio between the height and width of the table when you resize it, press and hold Shift while you drag to resize the table.

4- To keep the table centred on the slide, hold down Ctrl while you drag to resize the table.

ч- If you make the table too large for the slide, click Undo Bddin the Quick Access toolbar to restore the table to its original size.

ENTER A SPECIFIC TABLE SIZE

1. Click on the table to be resized.
2. Under **Table tools**, in the **Layout** tab , in the **Table size** group , enter the desired size in the **Height** and **Width** fields .

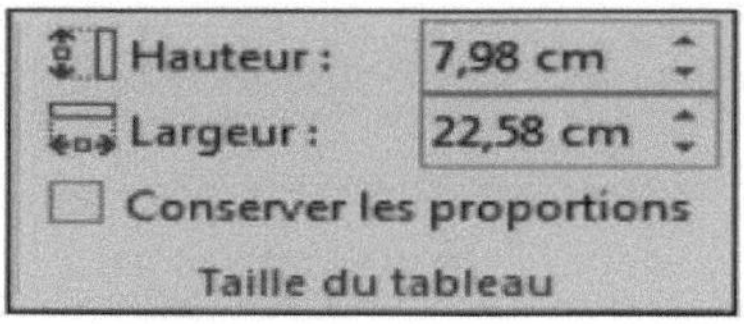

To maintain the same ratio between the height and width of the table when you resize it, activate the **Lock aspect ratio checkbox.**

MOVING A TABLE

1. Click on the table to be moved.
2. Place the pointer on the outermost border of the table (but not on the dots), then, when the pointer becomes an 'I', click and drag the border to move the table.

Tip: To move a table and create a duplicate, press and hold Ctrl while dragging the table.

III.4.ALIGNING A TABLE

To change the alignment, simply do the following:

1. Right-click the table you wish to align, then click **Table properties**.
2. In the **Table Properties** dialog box, click on the **table** tab.
3. Under **Horizontal Alignment**, click on the desired alignment .

111.5. FORMATTING A TABLE

1. Select the table.
2. Select the **Layout** tab.
3. To make changes, choose from the different groups:

- **Rows and columns**
- **Merge**
- **Cell size**
- **Alignment**
- **Table size**

111.6. ADVANCED FORMATTING

A. ADD TEXT

Press inside the space provided, then type or paste the text.

If your text exceeds the size of the reserved space, PowerPoint reduces the font size and line spacing incrementally as you type so that the text fits.

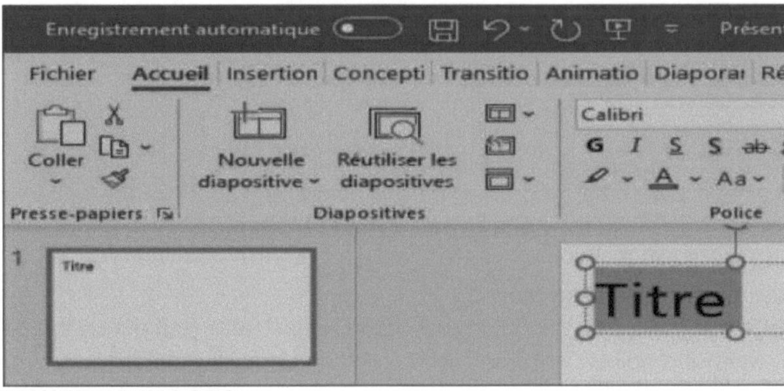

B. INSERTING IMAGES

1. Select the position where you want to insert the image on the slide.
2. In the **insertion** tab, select **images** or **online images**.
3. In the dialogue box that opens, find the image you want to insert, press it, then click **Insert**.

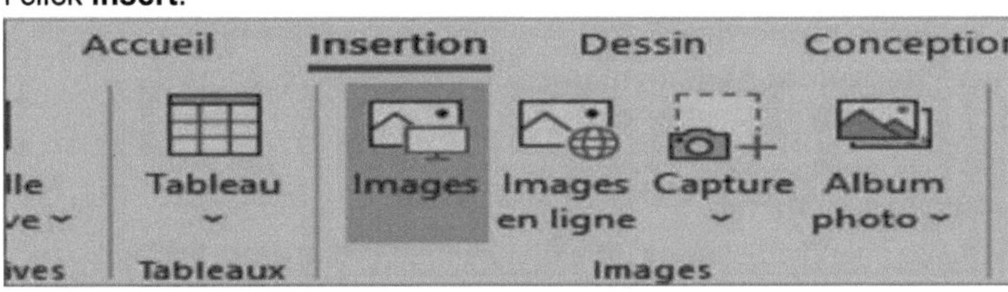

C. INSERTING SHAPES, ICONS, GRAPHICS AND SMARTART CHARTS

The **insertion** tab lets add a visual touch to your slides.

- Select **insert> shapes** , then, in the drop-down list, select the shape.
- In the drop-down menu, select **insert> icons** , then select the icon.
- Select **insert> SmartArt graphic**, then in the Gallery, press the SmartArt graphic layout of your choice.
- Select **insert>** , then click on the type of graph, then double-click on the graph you want.

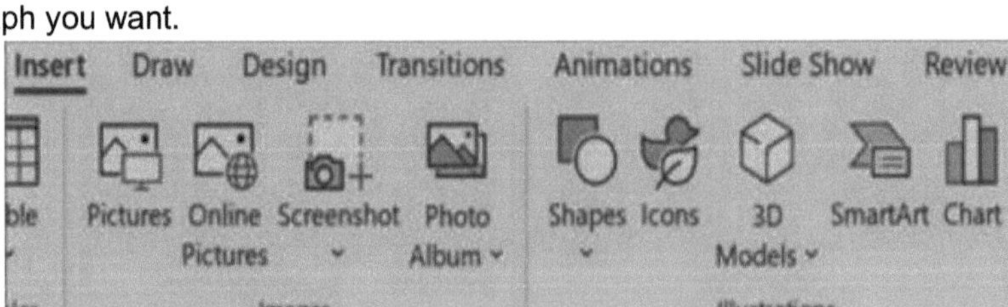

D. INSERTING VIDEOS

1. In your web browser, search for the video you want.

2. For an online video, copy the URL of the web page from the address bar of your browser.
3. Return to PowerPoint and select the slide on which you want to place the video.
4. In the **Insert** tab of the Ribbon, select **Video**> **Online video**.
5. In the **Online Video** dialog box, paste the URL you copied in step 2.
6. Select **Insert**.

CHAPTER IV

EXCEL CHART

Graph: a graph can be defined as a pictorial representation of the relationship between two or more variables containing quantitative values.[3]

Diagram: a diagram can be defined as a visual representation of any type of data in the form of a diagram, image or graph, and is intended to make information easier to understand.[4]

IV.1.DIFFERENT TYPES OF GRAPHICS

Data is the cornerstone of business efficiency. Without data, you can't get the information you need to get the job done. What's more, by quickly reading and analysing your data, you can understand how certain factors influence your overall success and proactive decision-making. That's why data visibility is so important. Creating a graph or diagram helps you (and other collaborators) to interpret the data and the underlying issues.

IV.1.1.AREA CHART

An area chart is used to display quantitative data. It is based on the curve chart (see definition below). The area between the axis and the curve is commonly highlighted using colours, textures and hatching. In most cases, the user will use the area chart to compare two or more values. A line graph is generally easier to read when there many values to display. This type of chart is particularly appropriate when you need to compare between 2 and 5 different values that change over time, such as a multi-year change in *Sales versus Costs*.

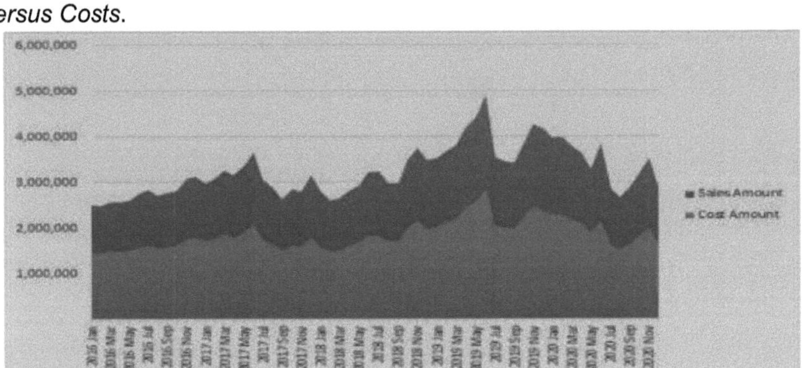

IV.1.2.BAR CHART

A bar chart presents grouped data in the form of rectangular bars, the lengths of which are proportional to the values they represent. The bars are arranged horizontally. A relevant use case for this type of chart is when you have

---

1 [3] https://www.voxco.com, consulted on 16/10/2023 at 04h31'.

[4] Ditto

comparative data organised into 10 or more categories, with long labels. For example, a graph of *Sales by representative*, where a large number of representatives are identified by their full name.

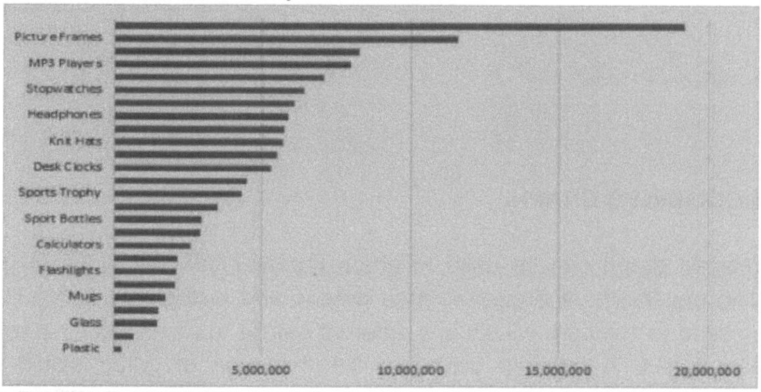

IV.1.3.BUBBLE CHART

Bubble charts are similar to scatter charts, but have an additional attribute. As with the scatter plot, two attributes indicate the X and Y positions of the bubble. Bubble charts add a third attribute which affects the size of the bubble. A use case for this type of chart would be, for example, to make a comparison between *costs and profits*, with the size of the bubble varying according to the percentage of overall sales.

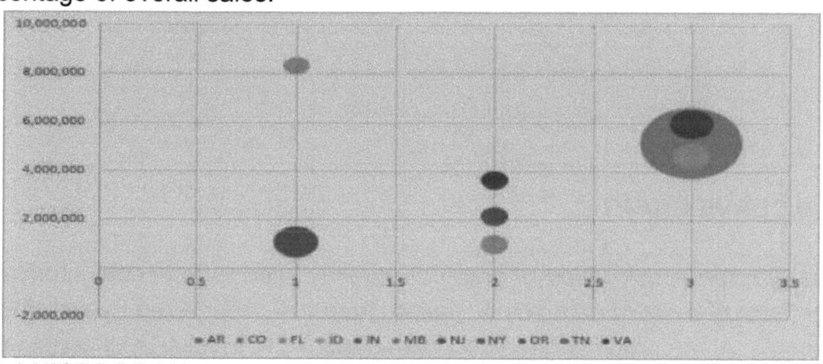

IV.1.4.HISTOGRAM

A histogram is a graphical representation of data. A histogram is presented in the form of successive vertical bars across the entire width of the graph, the values on the ordinate axis displayed on the left of the graph at . This type of chart is recommended for comparative data organised into 10 categories or less, with short labels. For example, a graph of *Sales by product category* without multiple categories and with relatively short names.

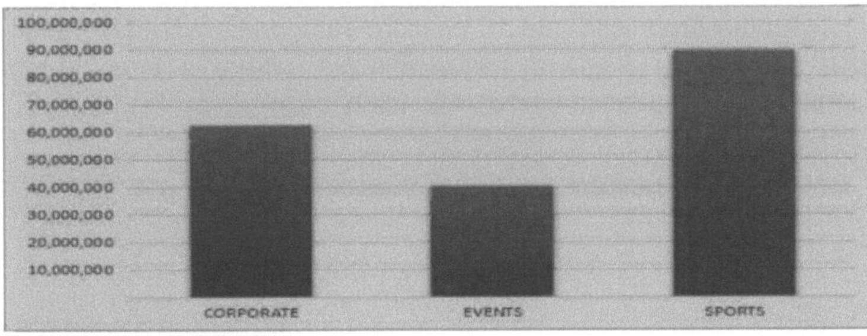

IV.1.5.COMBINED GRAPH

A combined graph can be used to group together different types of graph, including bar charts, line graphs, area graphs and histograms. If required, it can be used to compare values of a different nature, such as values in relation to percentages. A relevant use case for this type of graph would be a comparison between different types of values in the form of slightly different visual schemes. For example, a graph showing the *evolution of sales, costs and profit margins* over time might be used.
time.

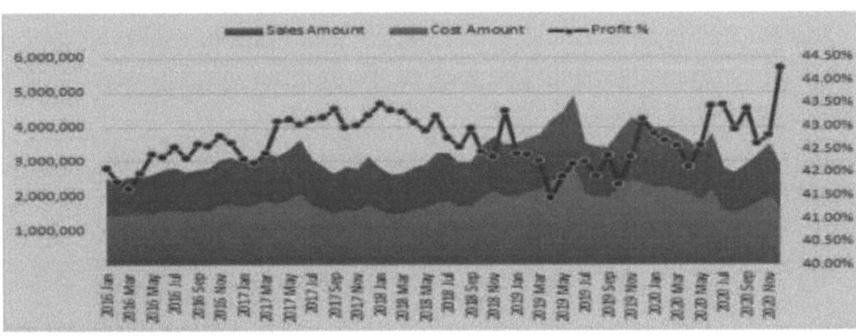

IV.1.6.CURVE CHART

A line graph is a basic type of graph, frequently used to represent information in the form of a set of data points, called "markers", connected by straight line segments. A line graph is often used to visualise the revolution of certain data over an interval of time, with the curve most often following a chronological order. This type of graph is recommended for comparing the revolution of several values, for example the *Quantities available per product category.*
over time.

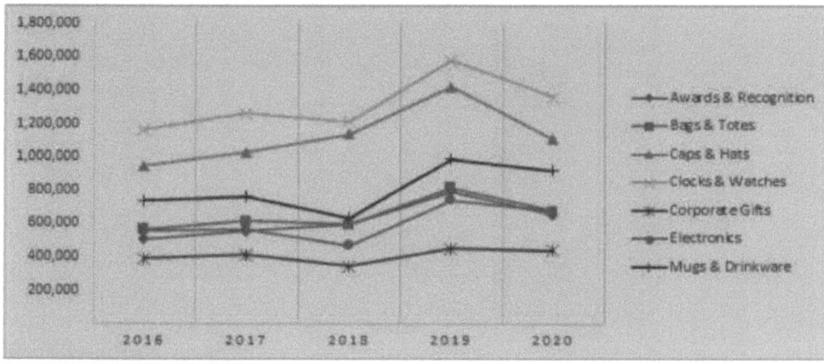

IV.1.8.SCATTER PLOTS

Also known as a scatter plot, this is a type of graph or mathematical diagram that uses cartesian coordinates to display the values of two variables for a set of data. If the points are colour-coded, you can increase the number of variables up to three. The data is displayed as a set of points, each with the value of one variable determining its position on the horizontal axis, and the value of the other variable determining its position on the vertical axis. A relevant use case would be to graphically represent the frequency of occurrence or total amounts on two dimensions, such as *Sales by state and product category*.

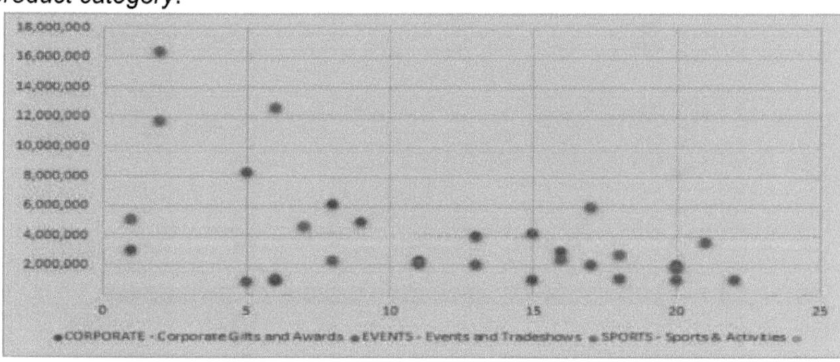

IV.1.9.SECTORAL GRAPHICS

A pie chart (also known as a pie graph or pie chart) is a statistical graph of circular shape, divided into parts, and illustrating a numerical proportion. In a pie chart, the arc length of each share, and therefore its central angle and area, are proportional to the quantity it represents. A pie chart can only display one set of data. Excel uses the identifier of this series as the chart title (e.g. "Flowers") and displays the values of this series in proportional parts on the pie chart. This type of chart is well suited to showing the distribution of a value within a dimension, such as *Sales per representative*.

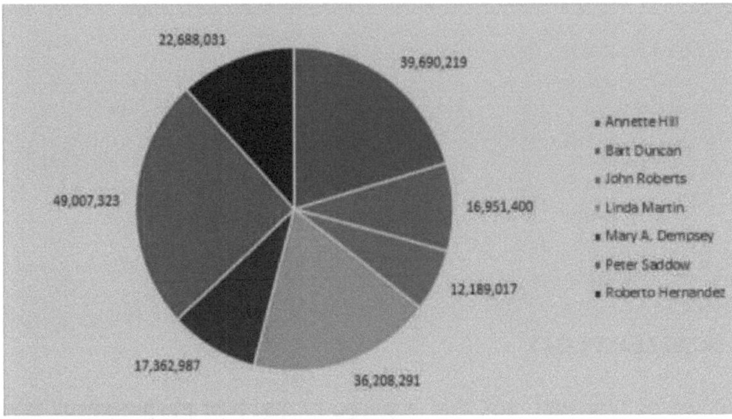

IV.1.10.VARIABLE-WIDTH HISTOGRAM

Also known as a Marimekko or Mekko chart, a variable-width histogram is a bar chart in which the width of the columns is adjusted so that the total width matches the desired width of the chart, with no gaps between the columns. This type of chart is useful for comparing how a value breaks down into percentages within a dimension.

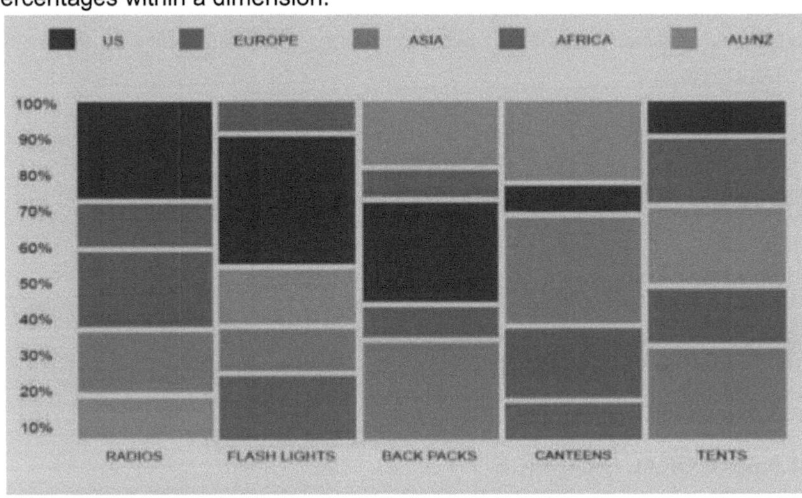

IV.1.11.3D AREA GRAPHICS

3D area charts display a revolution of values over a period or other category data, and use three editable axes (horizontal, vertical and depth). This type of chart is recommended for comparing the distribution of a value within a category and its chronological evolution, such as the *Evolution of sales by region*.

IV.1.12.STACKED AREA CHART

A stacked area graph displays a revolution of the contribution of each value over a given period or other categorical data. It is advisable to explain the stacked chart to users so that they can understand the values presented. A 3D stacked area chart is presented in the same way, but uses a 3D perspective and does not have a third axis. This type of chart is relevant for showing how different variables contribute to the total value over time.

IV.1.12.1.STACKED HISTOGRAM

Stacked histograms show the partial or complete relationship between different categories, and are therefore similar to stacked area charts. This type of chart requires at least two dimensional categories: one for stacked columns and one for comparison. This type of graph is relevant for showing how different portions contribute to the total value over time for a particular category.

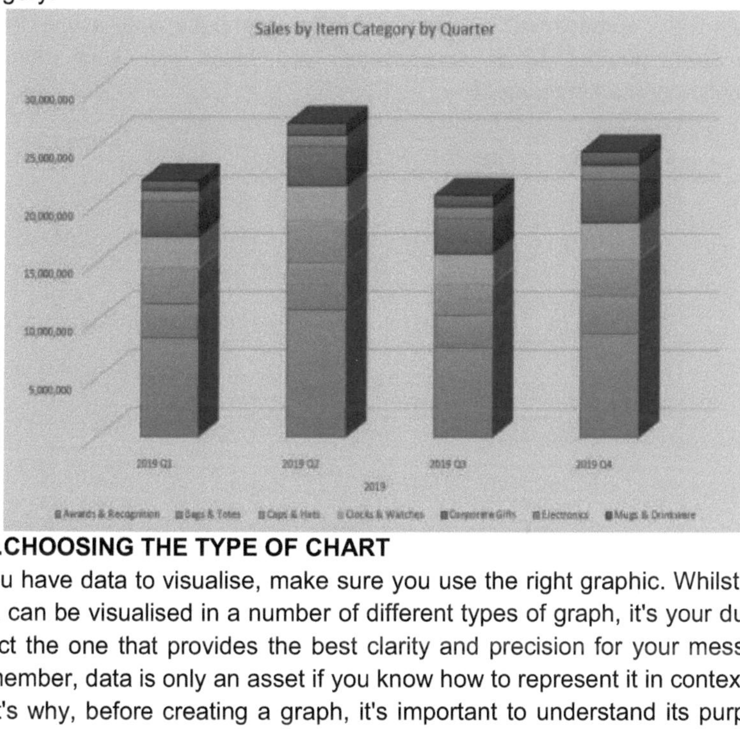

IV.2.CHOOSING THE TYPE OF CHART

If you have data to visualise, make sure you use the right graphic. Whilst your data can be visualised in a number of different types of graph, it's your duty to select the one that provides the best clarity and precision for your message. Remember, data is only an asset if you know how to represent it in context.

That's why, before creating a graph, it's important to understand its purpose. Graphs, maps and infographics help people to understand complex data, find patterns, identify trends and tell a story. Think about the message you want to convey to your audience

In conclusion, follow good graphic design practice, because your figures need to speak for themselves and your graphics need to adapt accordingly.

IV.3.RADAR CHART

To insert a radar chart in PowerPoint you must first open a blank presentation. Then go to the Insert menu and click on Chart. Here you can choose the type of chart before is inserted into the slide.

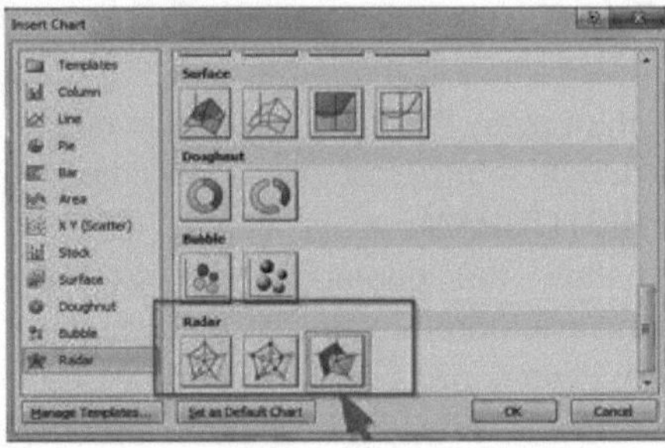

As you can see, there's a dedicated radar category. Here you can choose between three different radar maps in PowerPoint 2010.

Now an Excel spreadsheet will open where you can put in your actual data or paste from another Excel spreadsheet you have with your company information or market research.

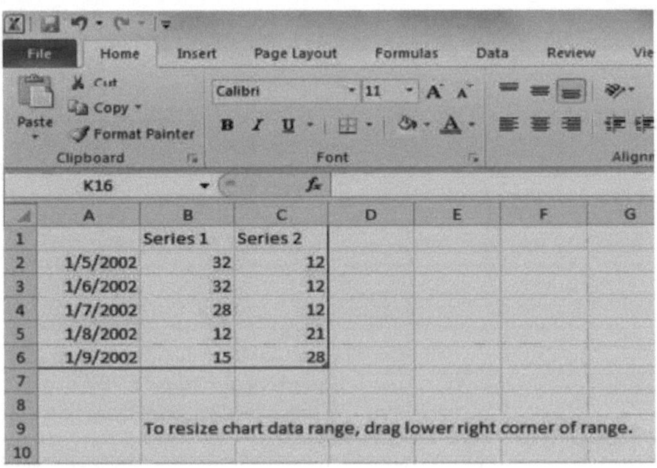

When you have finished, close Excel and the graph will appear. Here's an example:

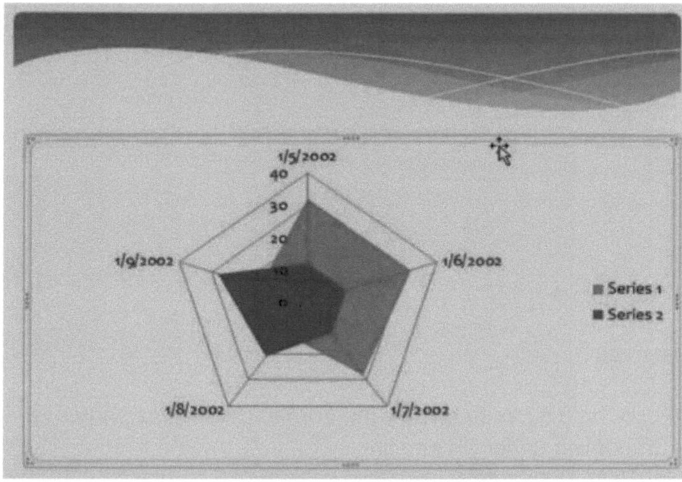

Radar charts are also known as Spider Charts because the representation is like a web with a spider. This type of chart visually compares several entities (e.g. products, organisations, investment opportunities, people, etc.) on several dimensions.

IV.4.GRAPH CURVE

To insert a Curve chart in an Excel sheet :

1. Select a cell in the data range or select the cells to be displayed in the graph.
2. Under the Insert / Charts tab, click on the Insert a line chart button.
3. Click on the model you want.

Click on the buttons to the right of the graph to customise it.

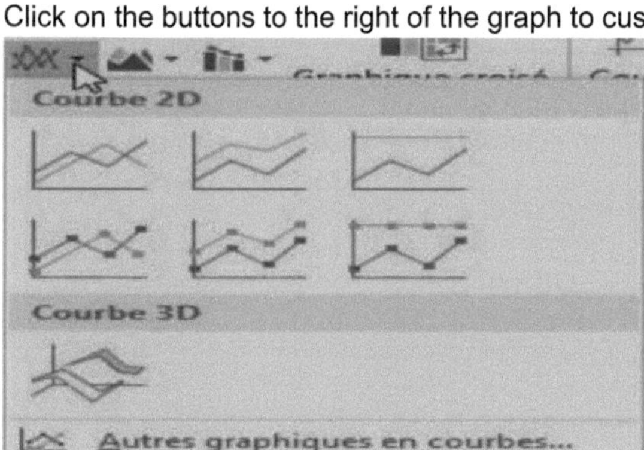

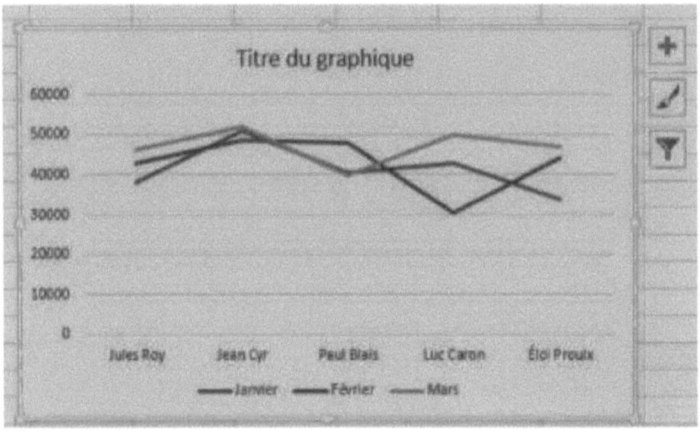

To round curves :

1. Double-click on a curve to display the Format data series pane.
2. Check Smoothing under Fill and line.

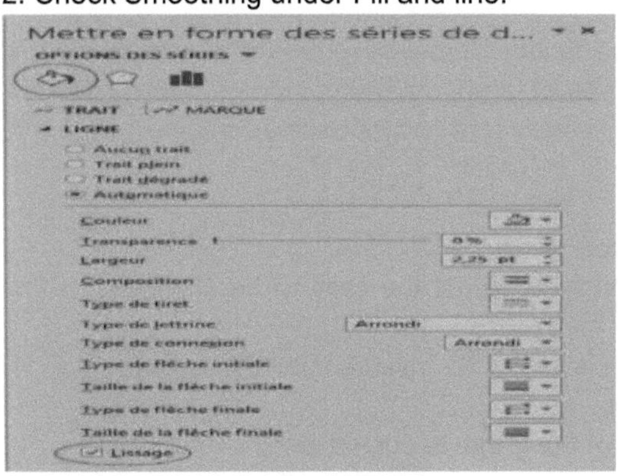

IV.5.MODIFYING DATA SERIES

To modify the data series, simply do the following;

1. Right-click on your graph, then **select Select data.**

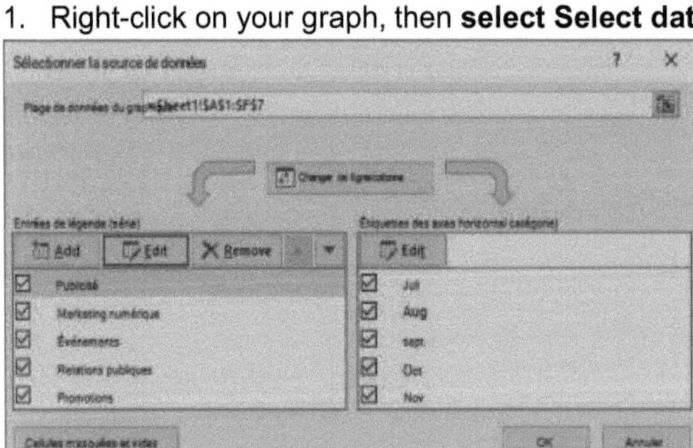

2. In the **Legend entry (Series)** area, click on the series you want to modify.
3. Click **Modify**, make the changes you want, then click **OK**.

The changes you make may interrupt the links with the data source on the spreadsheet.

4. To reorganise a series, select it, then click on Move to **IHJor** Move to LE. You can also add a series of data or delete them in this dialog box by clicking on Add **or Delete.** Deleting a data set removes it from the chart and you cannot use the chart filters to display it again.

If you want to rename a data set, see Rename a data set.

FILTERING DATA IN YOUR GRAPH

Let's start with the chart filters.

1. Click anywhere in the graph.
2. **Click on the** Chart **Filters button**.
3. Under the **Values** tab, tick or untick the series or categories you wish to show or hide.

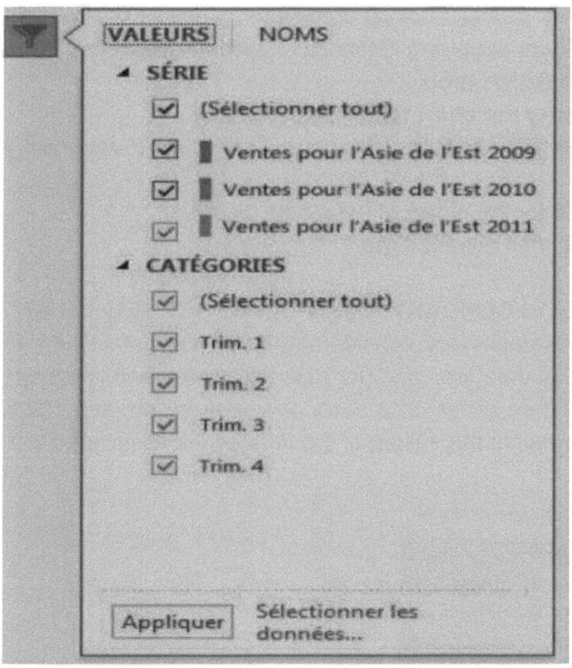

4. Click **Apply**.
5. If you wish to modify or reorganise the data in your series, click on **Select data**, and follow steps 2 to 4 in the next section .

IV.6.TWO-AXIS COMBINATION CHARTS

When the numbers in a graph vary considerably from data series to data series, or when you have mixed data types (price and volume), plot one or more data series on a secondary vertical (value) axis. The scale of this axis displays the values of the data series associated with it. A secondary axis works well in a graph displaying a combination histograms and line graphs.

You can quickly display a chart like this by changing your chart to a combination chart.

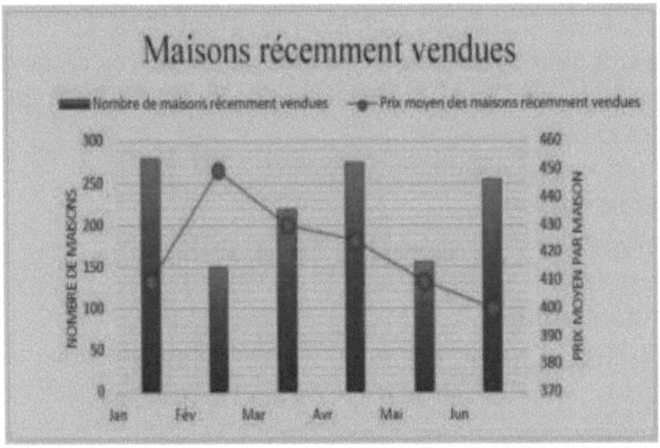

Note: The following procedure applies to Office 2013 and later versions.

1. Select a graph to open **Graph tools**.
2. Select **Creation> Modify the chart type**.
3. Select **Graphics combine> Histogram group - curve on a secondary axis**.
4. Select **Secondary axis** for the series of data to be displayed.
5. Select the down arrow, then choose **Line**.
6. Select **OK**.

ADDING OR DELETING A SECONDARY AXIS IN AN OFFICE 2010 CHART

When the values in a 2D graph vary considerably from one data series to another, or different types of data are used (for example, prices and volumes), you can plot one or more data series on a secondary vertical (ordinate) axis. The scale of this axis represents the values of the data series associated with it.

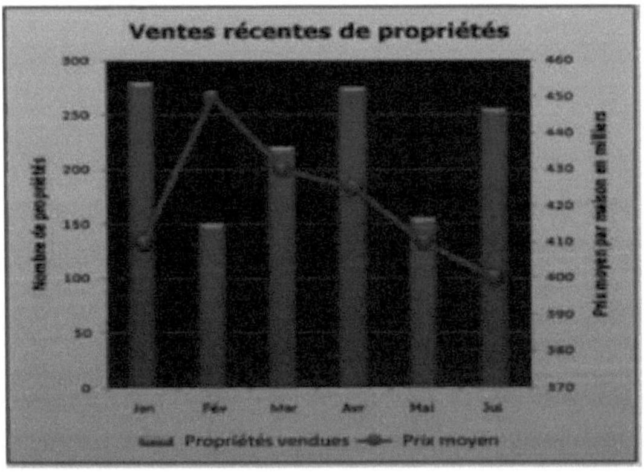

After adding a secondary vertical axis to a 2D chart, you can also add a secondary horizontal axis (x-axis), which can be useful in a scatter plot or bubble chart.

To better distinguish the data series plotted on the secondary axis, you can change their graph type. For example, in a histogram, you can convert the data series on the secondary axis into a line graph.

IV.7.GRAPHIC MODELS

Graph templates are used to format graphs. Graph templates can be used to configure a number of presentation parameters, including the size of the ordinate axis, the width and height of the graph and the different colours...

CHAPTER V

IMPORTING POWERPOINT GRAPHICS

V.1.INSERTING A GRAPHIC

You can create a chart in PowerPoint or Excel. If your chart is based on a lot of data, create it in Excel, then copy it into your presentation. This is also the best solution if your data changes frequently and your chart needs to be kept up to date. In this case, when you copy and paste the chart, link it to the original Excel file.

To create a simple graph from scratch in PowerPoint, click on **Insert>** **Graph**, then select the graph you want.

1. Click on **Insert>** **Graphics**.

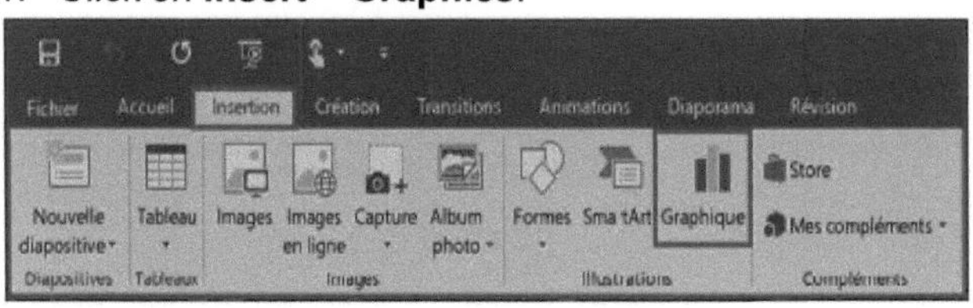

2. Click on the chart type, then double-click on the chart would like to see.

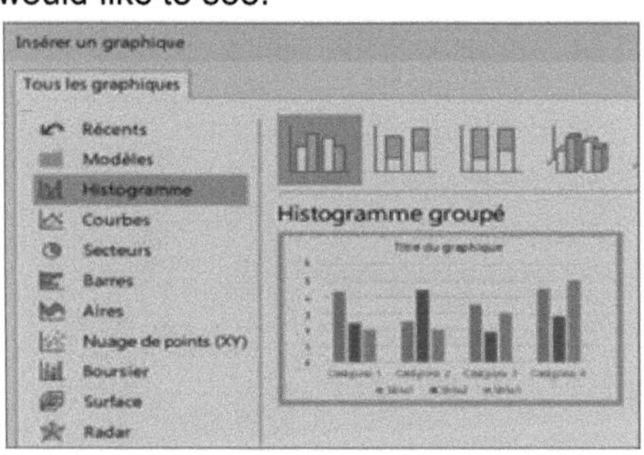

3. In the spreadsheet that opens, replace the data for the reserved spaces with your own information.

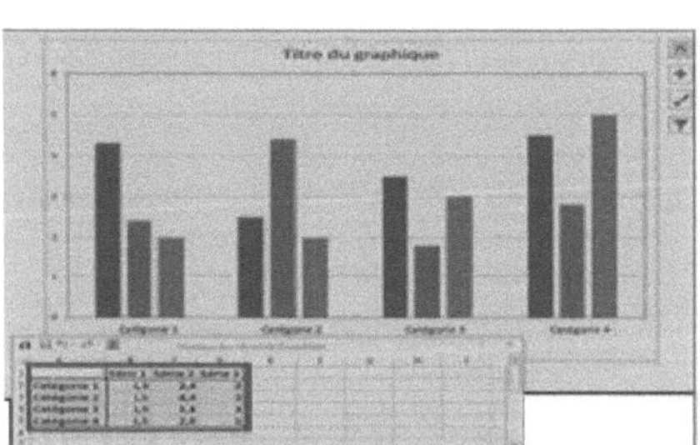

When you insert a graph, small buttons appear in the top right-hand corner.

Use the **Chart elements** button to display, hide or format elements such as axis titles or data labels. Or use the **Chart Styles** button is a more advanced option that displays or hides the data in your chart.

4. When you have finished, close the worksheet.

V.2.FORMATTING A GRAPH

Select the chart element (for example, data series, axes or titles), right-click on it and then click **Format <chart element>** . The **Format** pane is displayed with options tailored to the selected chart element.

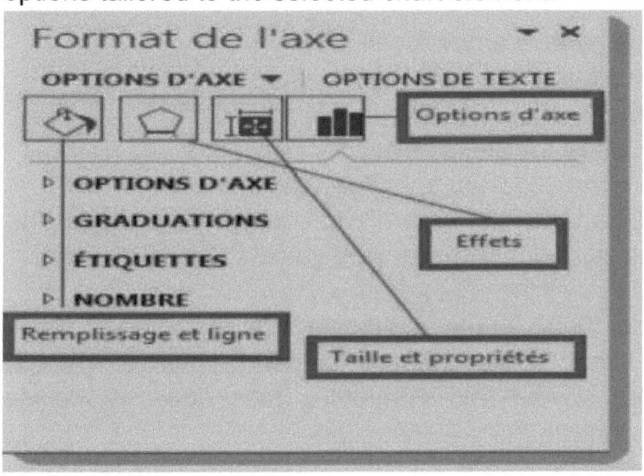

Clicking on the small icons at the top of the pane takes you to other parts of the pane with more options. If you click on another chart element, you'll see that the Office pane automatically updates to the new chart element.

For example, to format an axis :

1. Right-click on the graph axis, then click **Format axis.**

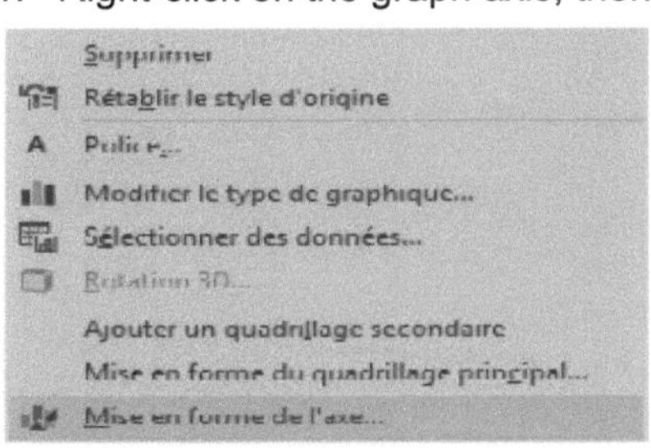

2. In the Office **Axis Format** pane, make the following changes desired.

You can move or resize the Office pane to make it easier to use. Click on the chevron in the top right-hand corner.

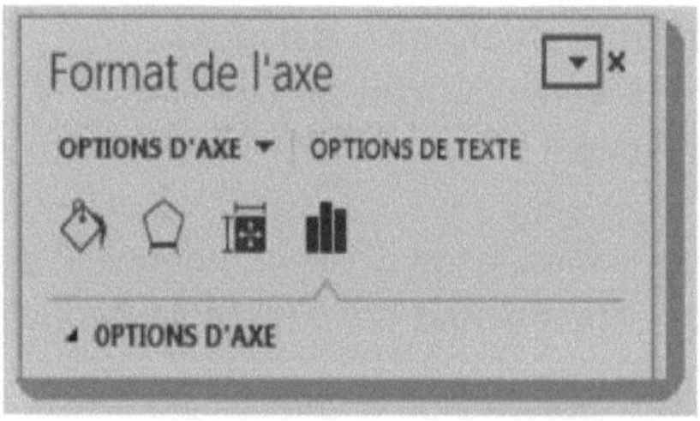

o Select **Move**, then drag the pane to a new location.
o Select **Size**, then drag the edge of the pane to resize it.

V.3.DATA MODIFICATION

To modify the data, simply follow the steps below:

1. On the slide, select the chart you want to modify. **The** Chart **Tools contextual tab** appears at the top of the PowerPoint chart. If you don't see the Chart **Tools** tab or Creation tab below it, make sure you click on the chart to select it.

Note: The Design tab under Chart **Tools** is different from the default Design tab in PowerPoint. **The** Chart **Tools tab** only appears when a chart is selected, and the **Design,** Layout and Formatting tabs under it provide different commands related only to the selected chart.

2. Under Chart **tools**, on the Creation **tab**, in the Data **group**, click on Modify **data.**

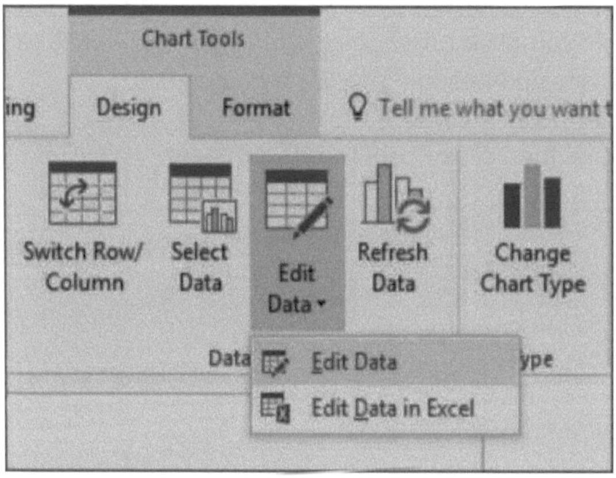

3. You have done one of the following:

- To modify the data in PowerPoint data, click **on Modify data.** A spreadsheet window will open.

Note: If the classes you are working on have specific start-up requirements, such as content activation, you must also do this in the window.

- To modify the data directly in Excel, click **on Modify data in Excel.**
- Make the changes you want. They will be reflected in the graphic in PowerPoint.

CHAPTER VI

USE OUTLOOK APPLICATION EXERCISE

Outlook is a program in the Microsoft Office suite that lets you receive and send emails, file them, manage a full address book and manage your tasks and time. In the office, Outlook can be connected so that you can check other people's availability to make appointments.

VI.1.TIMETABLE

To create a calendar with Outlook, follow these steps :

1. In **Outlook**.com, select Calendar. > Add a calendar > **Create a calendar**.
2. Give your calendar a name.
3. Personalise your calendar with a colour, a charm or both.
4. Optional: add your calendar to an existing calendar group.
5. Select Save.

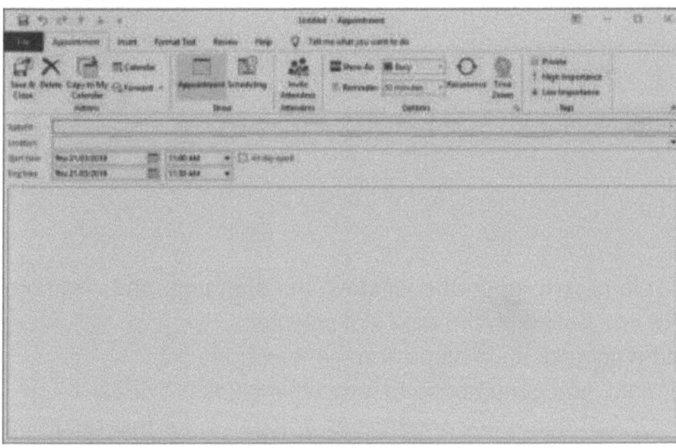

VI.2.CREATING APPOINTMENTS

To create a recurring appointment, follow these steps:

1. Open **Microsoft Outlook**
2. In the folders pane, select Calendar

3. Locate the day and time in the Calendar view where you want to add a recurring appointment. Click once on it with the left mouse button.

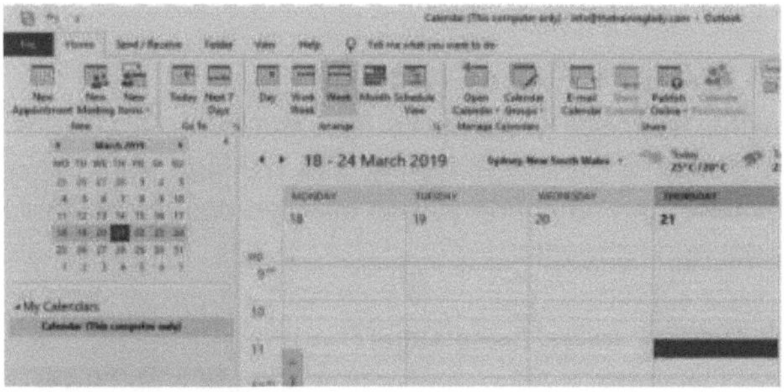

4. A blue bar will appear
5. Double-click on the time slot to open the Untitled window - Appointment :

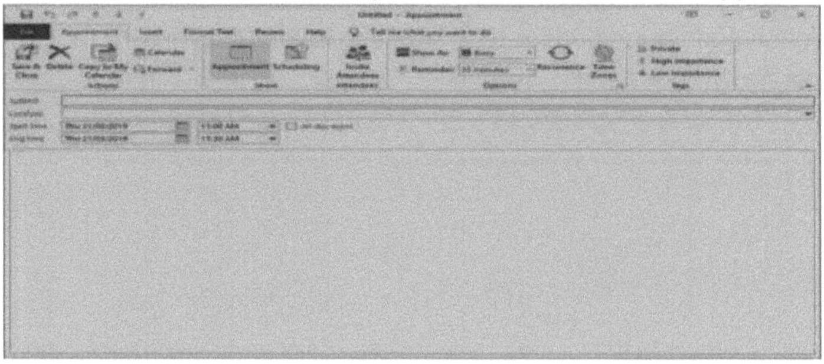

6. By using the double-click to open the window, the start time and end time have been filled in for you based on the time slot selected.
7. You can now add a subject, such as paying the telephone bill.
8. In the "Location" field, you can choose to leave this blank if it doesn't apply to the appointment. Or you can enter an address or location for this recurring appointment.
9. Make sure that the start time and end time are correct for the date and time. If not, simply click on the calendar icon to adjust the dates.
10. Next, you need to choose how to display this period in the calendar. Is it simply that you'll be busy or that you won't be in the office?

RECURRENCE

1. Now click on the Recurrence button on the Ribbon.
2. The Appointment recurrence dialog box appears.

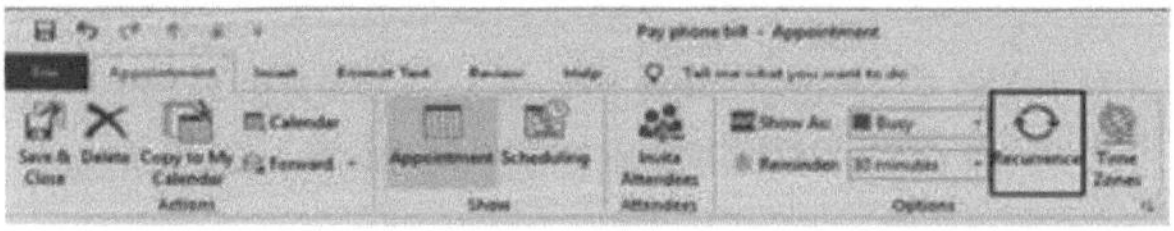

3. The Appointment recurrence dialog box appears.

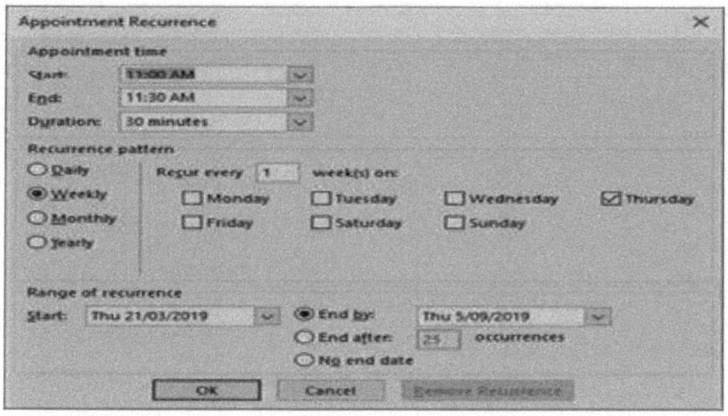

4. You can now specify a recurrence pattern, for example daily, weekly, monthly or yearly. I'll choose Monthly
5. You can now choose whether you want the appointment to always take place on the same day of the month or whether it should take place every third Tuesday. I select day 21 of each month.
6. Next, you can specify the recurrence range. Do you want the appointment to continue indefinitely in your calendar or should it stop after a certain number occurrences? Choose from the following options
7. Click OK to return to the appointment window
8. The details of the recurrence now appear in the window.

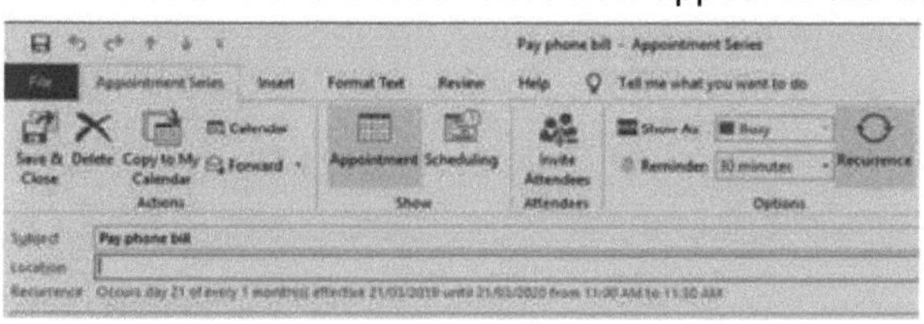

9. Now click on Save and close in the ribbon
10. Move forward in your calendar to the next date on which your appointment is due to take place and make sure that it appears in your calendar.
11. You have now created a recurring appointment

CONCLUSION

You will now see your recurring appointment in your calendar in the period you have specified. By default, you will also receive a reminder on the same day via the reminders window. Click here for more articles about Microsoft Outlook.

VI.3.CREATING AND MODIFYING TASKS

VI.3.1.CREATING TASKS

If you want to plan your activity efficiently, use Outlook's task system. This will allow you to set deadlines and keep track of your activities.

IIn **Outlook 2013 and 2010**, click on *New items*, then *Task*.

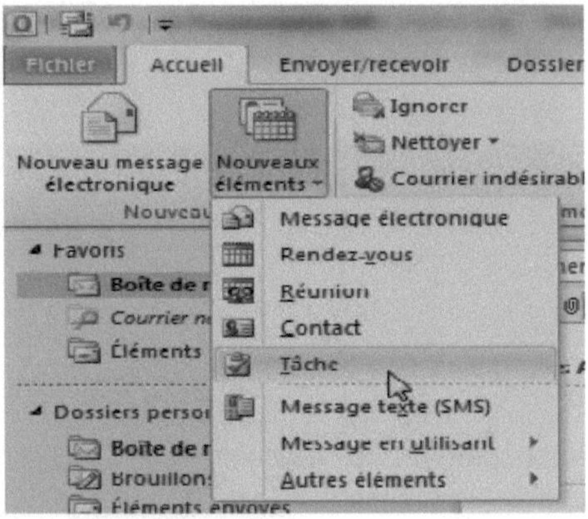

In **other versions**, click on the small arrow to the right of the *New* button on the toolbar, then select *Spot*.

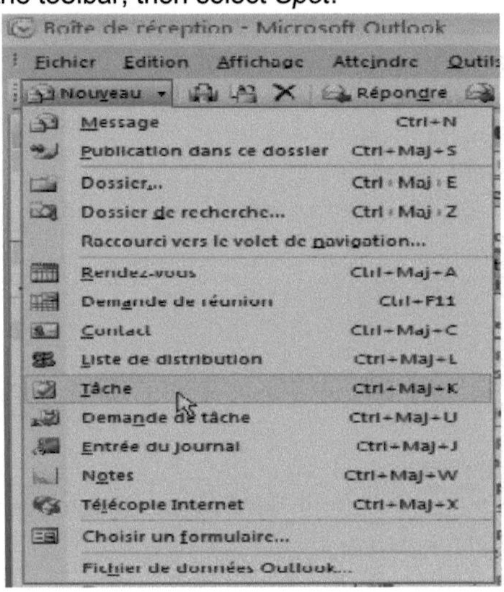

In the window that opens, type the name of the task in the *Subject* field, then specify the start date (if required) and the due date.

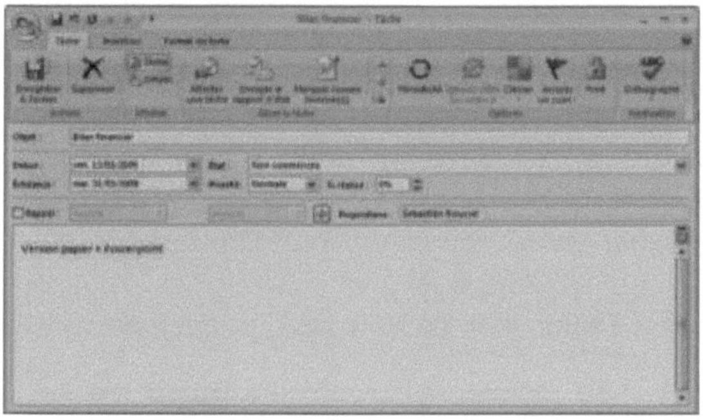

You can also specify the status of the task (*Not started, In progress, Completed, Waiting for someone else* or *Postponed),* the priority (*Low, Normal* or *High)* and finally the percentage completed.

You can also type the details in the box at the bottom of the window.

OPTIONS :

- In the latest versions Outlook, you can **classify your task** by clicking on the *Classify* button (in Outlok 2007) or *Categories* (in other versions).
- By ticking the *Remind* box, you can ask Outlook to **remind you of the task** on a date in the future of your choice.
- To **assign the task to someone else**, click on the *Assign a task* button (or *Assign a task*) and select the relevant contacts in field *a*.
- By clicking on *Details* button or tab, you can **enter details** of the work carried out, such as working time, mileage or invoicing information.

Finally, click on the *Save and Close* button to finish.

TO MANAGE STAINS

To display the list of tasks, display the Outlook *Tasks* module: click on the appropriate icon in the navigation pane.

Simply tick a task to indicate that it has been completed.

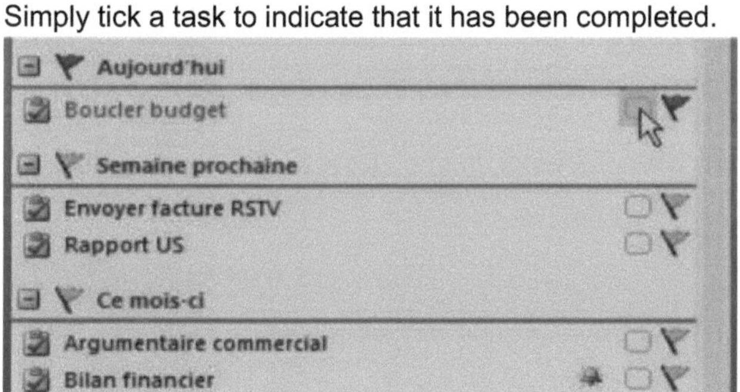

VI.3.2.MODIFYING A TASK

It is sometimes necessary to modify a task, for example, to change the percentage completion, the due date or to add notes on the work done.

1. In the task list pane, double-click on the task to be modified. This action will open the task window.
2. Make the necessary changes.
3. In the **Home** tab, **Actions group**, click **Save and close.**

VI.4.ASSIGNMENT OF TASKS

Tasks help you keep track of your tasks. You can also assign tasks to other people.

1. In the navigation bar, click on **Tasks**, then on **New task**, or open an existing task.
2. Click **on Assign a task.**

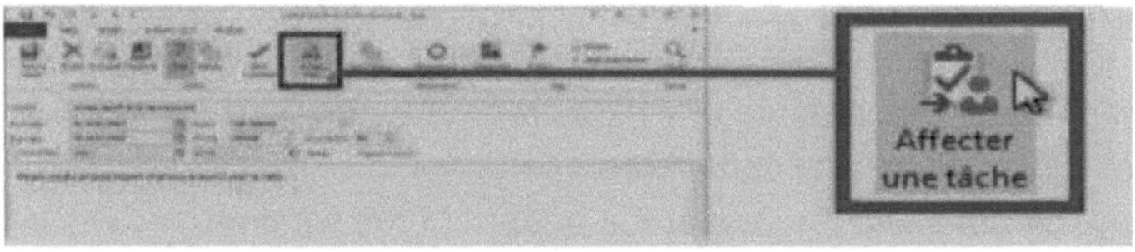

3. In the **To** field, enter a name or an e-mail address.
4. Enter **the subject,** start date and **expiry** date.

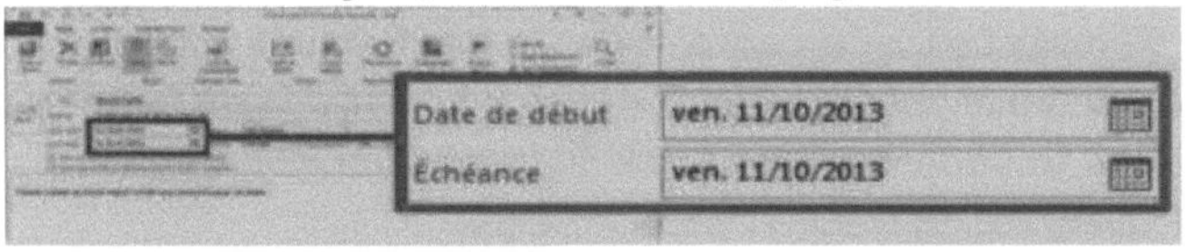

5. If you want the task to be repeated, click **Recurrence**, select the options you want, then click **OK.**
6. Click on **Send**.

Note: If you assign a periodic task, a copy of that task remains in your task list but is never updated. If you tick in the **Send** status **report** when completed box, you will receive status reports for each completed instance of the task.

VI.5.ASSIGNMENT OF TASKS

Tasks help you keep track of your tasks. You can also assign tasks to other people.

1. In the navigation bar, click on **Tasks**, then on **New task**, or open an existing task.
2. Click **on Assign a task.**

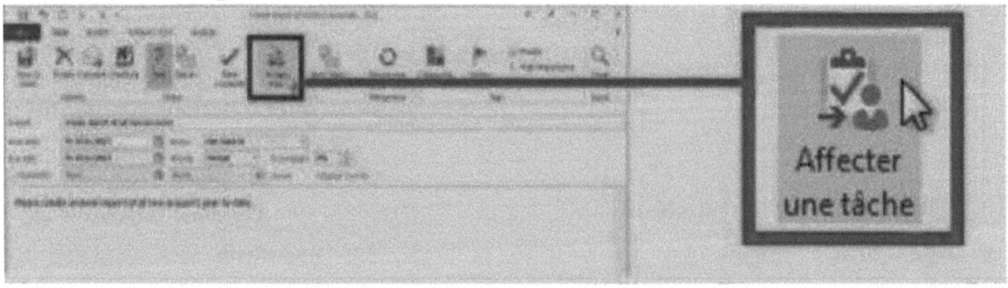

3. In the **To** field, enter a name or an e-mail address.
4. Enter **the subject,** start date and **expiry** date.

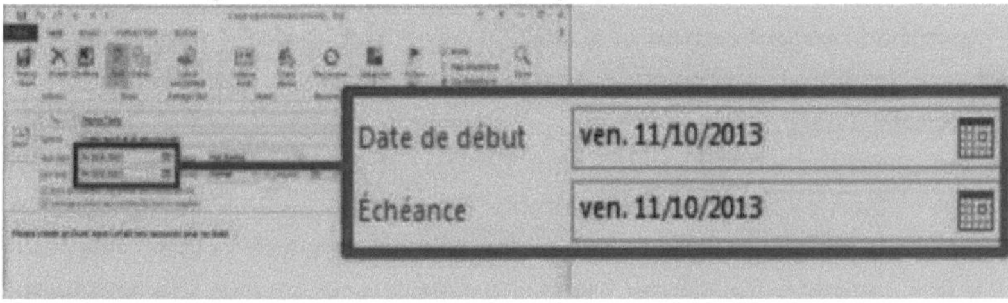

5. If you want the task to recur, click **Recurrence**, select the options you want, then click **OK.**
6. Click on **Send**.

Note: If you assign a periodic task, a copy of that task remains in your task list but is never updated. If you check the **Send** status **report** when completed box, you will receive status reports for each completed instance of the task.

CHAPTER VII

POWERPOINT ANIMATIONS

In Powerpoint**, an animation** is a special effect applied to a single element of a slide, such as text, a shape, an image, etc .[5]

VII.1.TRANSITION

A *transition* is the special effect that occurs when you leave one slide and move on to the next during a presentation.

A transition is an effect used to link slides and give rhythm to the presentation. A real link between the slides, transition effects ensure that the presentation flows smoothly. Be careful not to confuse transition and animation; these are two effects which influence the flow of the slideshow, but a transition affects the entire slide an animation affects an object on the slide. A slide can therefore have one transition and contain several objects, each with one or more animations.

INSERT A TRANSITION

To insert and set a transition, click on the 'Transitions' tab.

There are 3 steps to inserting a transition:

1. **Select** the slide on which you want to apply the transition.
2. To place a transition, select the **'Transition to this slide' group** and then use the list to display the proposed transitions.
3. **Choose the type of transition** you want. To test the effect, place the mouse over one of the proposed transitions without clicking; to choose the transition and assign it to the slide, click on it.

To rectify an error or cancel a transition, click on 'None'.
(top left).

[5] https://support.microsoft.com, consulted on 17/10/2023 at 08h39'.

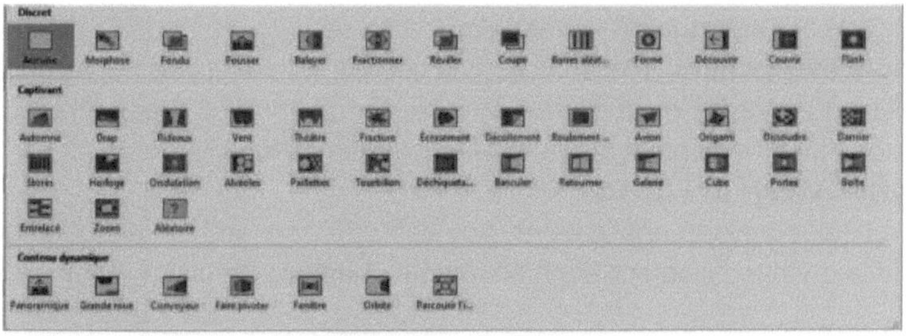

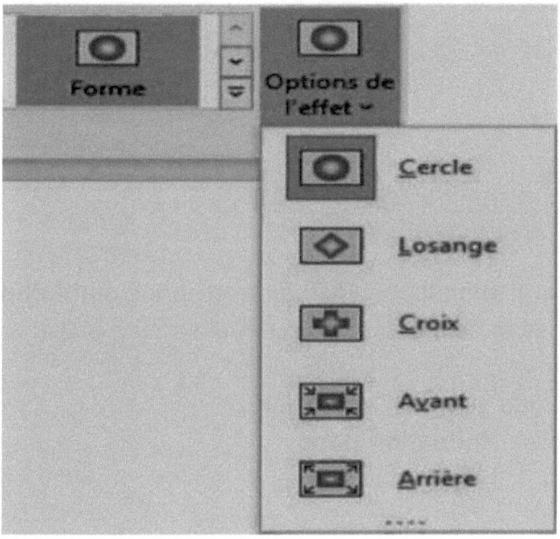

Some transitions have variants; these differ depending on the transition chosen. To choose from the available variants, click on Effect options to discover the different options.

SETTING UP A TRANSITION

NB You can test the transition at any time by clicking on Aperpu.

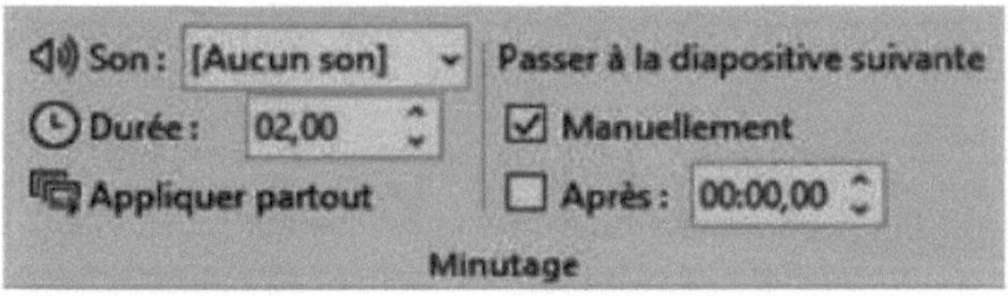

Various parameters can be applied to a transition to personalise it.

- **Sound**: this option lets you choose a sound to accompany the transition; be careful, if you have chosen an audio clip to accompany this slide, you will end up with an overlay of sounds.
- **Duration:** each transition has an initial duration by default; this can be modified. Use the arrows to increase or decrease it.
- **Move on to the next slide**: for a slideshow, tick 'After:' and specify a duration in seconds. In this case, the presentation will run without user

intervention but after the predefined time.

- **Apply everywhere**: The settings you choose will be applied to all slides.

NB: clicking on 'Apply everywhere' must be done after the other settings, if you want the settings you have made to be applied to all the slides.

VII.2.ANIMATION EFFECTS

In PowerPoint desktop applications, you can apply several animation effects to a single text string or object, such an image, shape or SmartArt graphics file.

Tip: When working with several animation , you can work in the **Animation pane**, where you can see a list of all the animation effects on the active slide.

Open the Animation pane

1. Select the object on the slide you wish to animate.
2. In the **Animations** tab, click **Animation pane**.

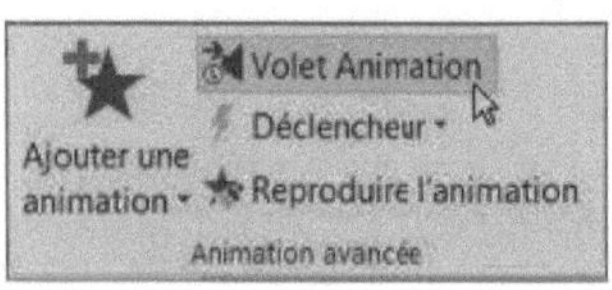

3. Click on **Add an animation**, then select an animation effect.

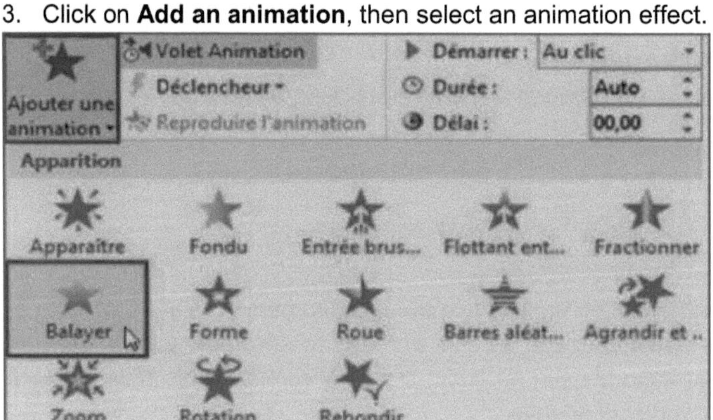

4. To apply additional animation effects to the same object, select it, click **Add animation**, then select another.

Important: Once you have applied the first animation effect, you will not be able to add *any further effects* without using the **Add animation** option. Otherwise, you will simply replace the existing effect with the one you want to add.

DEFINING THE START AND DURATION OF AN ANIMATION EFFECT

If you want to control the timing of animation effects, proceed as follows for each effect:

1. In the **Animation pane**, click the down arrow next to the animation, then click **Timing**.

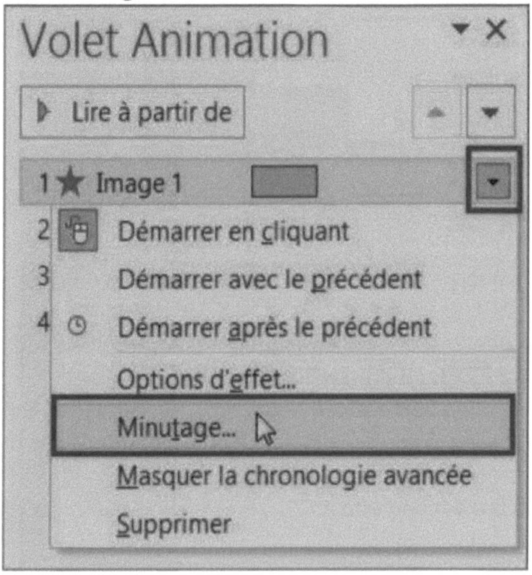

2. In the **Timing** tab, click the down arrow **Debut**, then choose one of the following options:
3. To start the animation by clicking with the mouse, choose **On click**.
4. To run the animation *at the same time as* the previous one, choose **With previous**.
5. To start the animation after the previous one, choose **After the previous one**.

Tip: The **previous** animation effect is the one listed in the playback order of the **Animation pane** (and is usually located just above the animation whose timing you are adjusting).

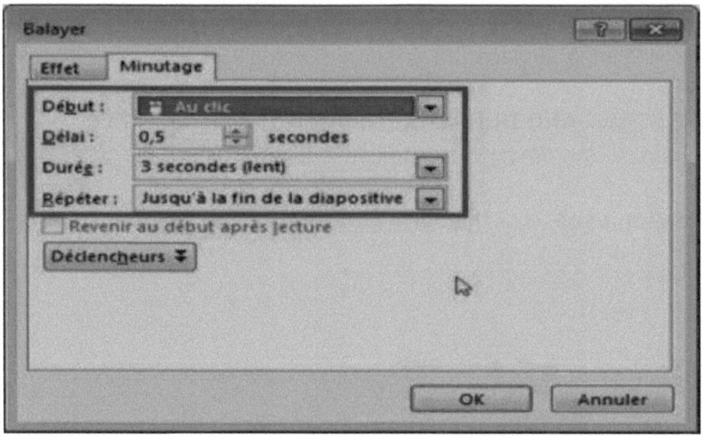

1. To delay the start of the animation effect, click **Delay**, then choose the number of seconds you want.
2. To change the speed of animation effects, set the **duration** to the desired value.
3. For a preview of animation effects, click on **Aperqu** in the **Animations** tab.

PLAY SEVERAL ANIMATION EFFECTS AT THE SAME TIME

You can make two or more animation occur at the same time for an object. For example, an image can fade *in and* float. To achieve this superimposition of two (or more) effects at once, proceed as follows

1. Use **Add animation** to add the second effect.

2. To synchronise the second effect, set **Start** to **With precedent**.

TIP FOR USING SEVERAL ANIMATION EFFECTS

When working with several objects on a slide, it can be difficult to distinguish between the objects and the animation effects applied to them.

In the illustration below, the default object names are not very explicit. It is therefore difficult to know which animation is being applied to which object.

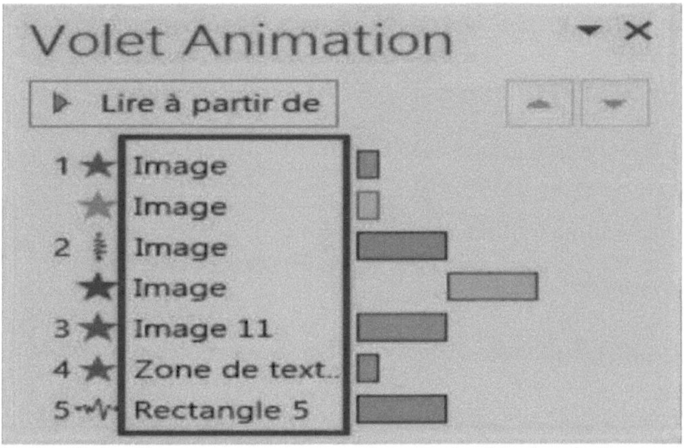

In the **Selection pane**, you can give each object a distinct name to make it easier to use when you apply animations to it. See below:

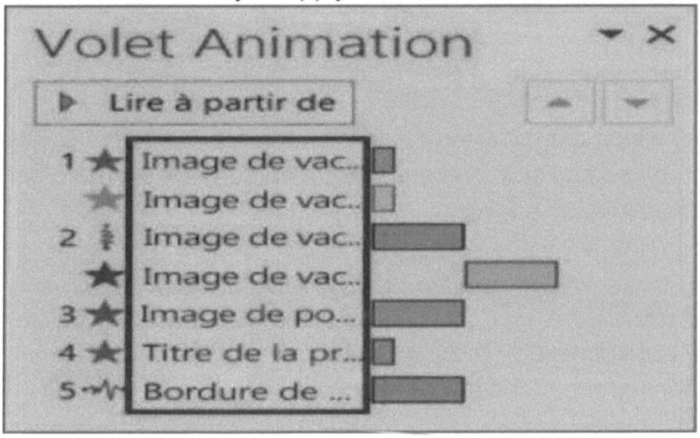

1. To change the default names of objects, on the **Home** tab, click on **Select**, then on **Selection pane**.

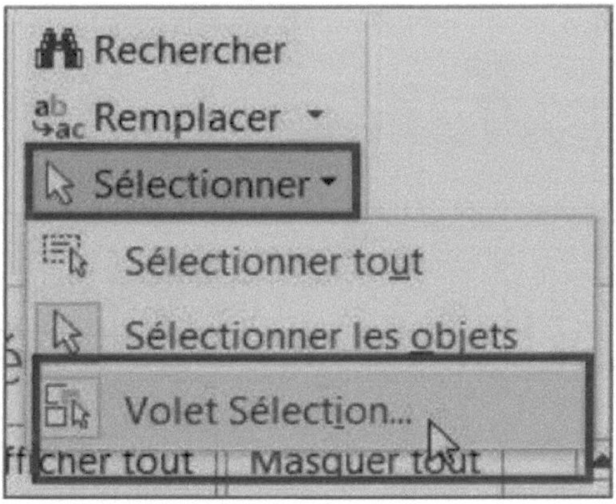

2. In the **Selection pane**, double-click on the object's default name to open the zone, then rename it.

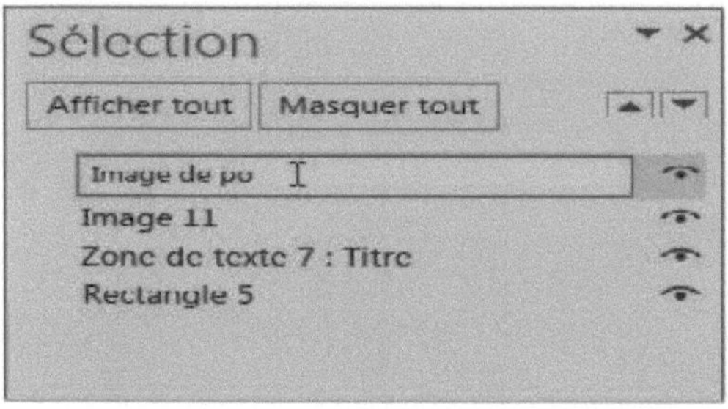

VII.3.EVENTS

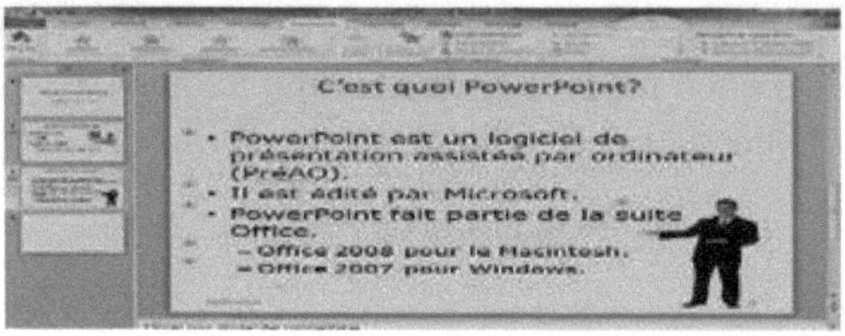

The animations pane, which can be used for text and image animations, lets control the animations by adding start and end effects and organising the order in which text or animated images appear.

The animations pane is displayed by clicking on the animations pane button in the advanced animations group of the animations tab.

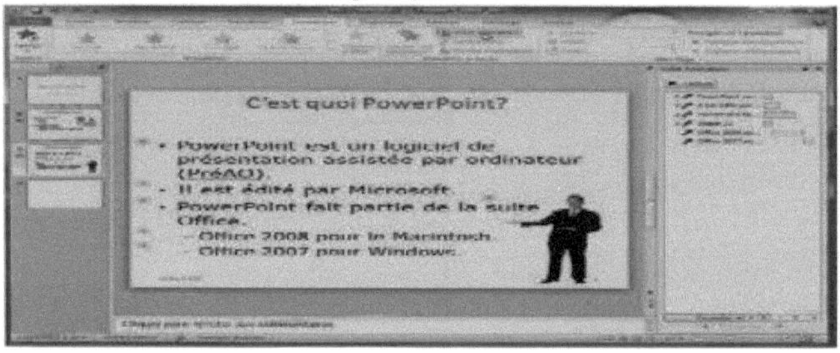

The animations pane is displayed to the right of the active slide; to make it disappear, click on the cross at the top right of the animations pane.

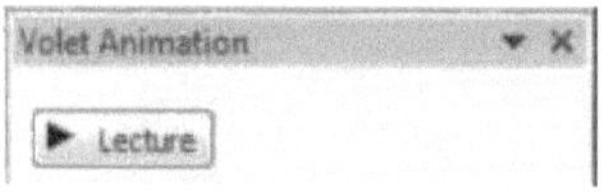

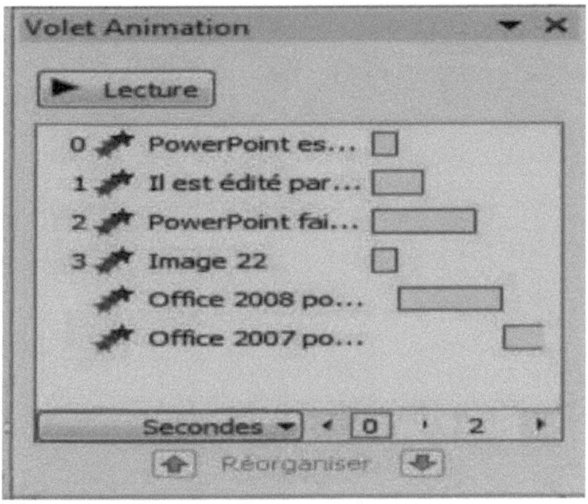

The animations section contains:

- A play button for visual control of the various animations.
- The different text and image animations ;
- Each animation has a number which indicates the order in which the animations appear.
- The number 0 means that text or image will be visible when the slide is displayed;
- Numbers 1 to n indicate that the animation will be controlled by an action (usually a click) or will be automatic (after the previous animation or at the same time);
- At the bottom is the time in seconds when the text or image appears;
- The reorganised arrows can be used to change the order of the animations.

0 - PowerPoint is computer-assisted presentation software (PreAO).

- It is ëditë by Microsoft.
- PowerPoint is part of the

Here the PowerPoint text is... has level zero and will be displayed when the slide is displayed (start with the previous one).

To find out more about an animation.

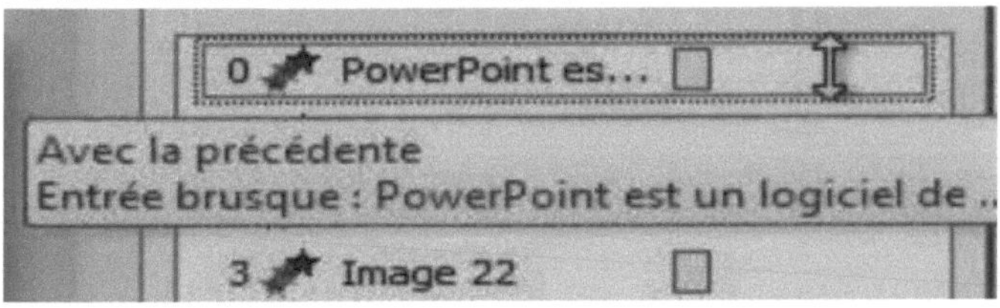

To find out more about an animation, click on it in the animations pane. A double arrow appears, allowing you to change the order the animations appear (as we shall see later).

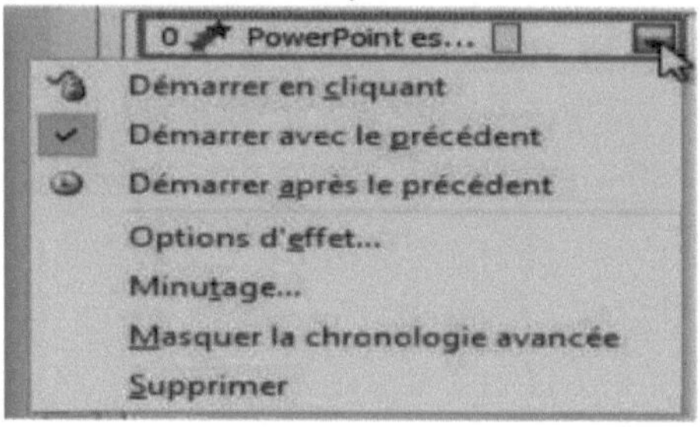

Click in the rectangle to reveal a small triangle, then a drop-down menu giving access to additional information and functions.

MODIFY ANIMATIONS.

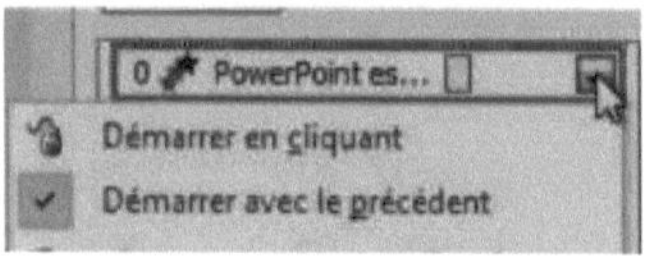

The text is edited... has level 1 and the appearance of the text will be controlled
(with a click).

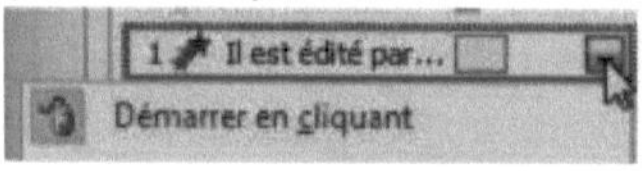

The PowerPoint text does... has level 2 and the text will appear controlled (by a click).

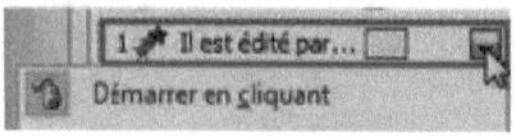

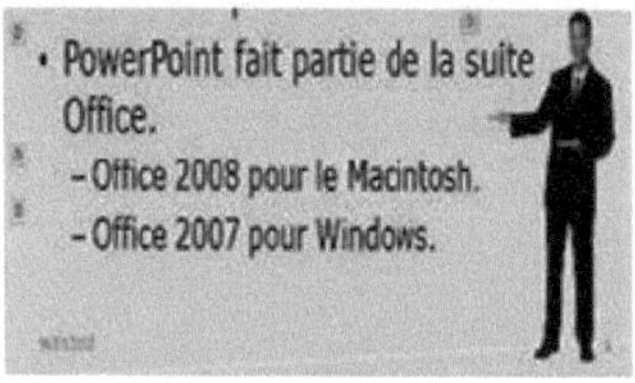

The image on the right (the smiling presenter, image 22) and the texts Office 2008... and Office 2007... Have level 3 and the appearance of the image and text will be controlled.

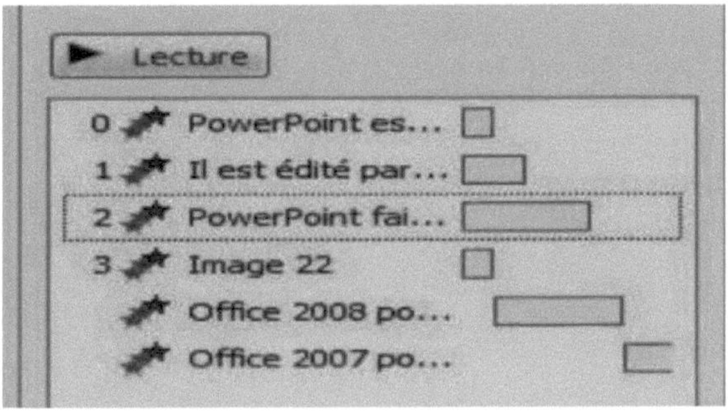

The small orange rectangle indicates the display time of the text or image.

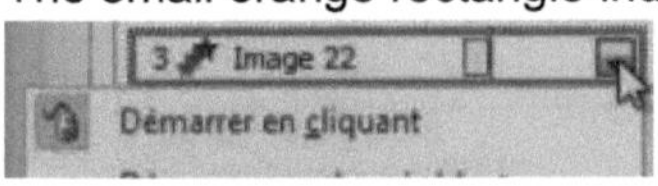

The image appears with a click.

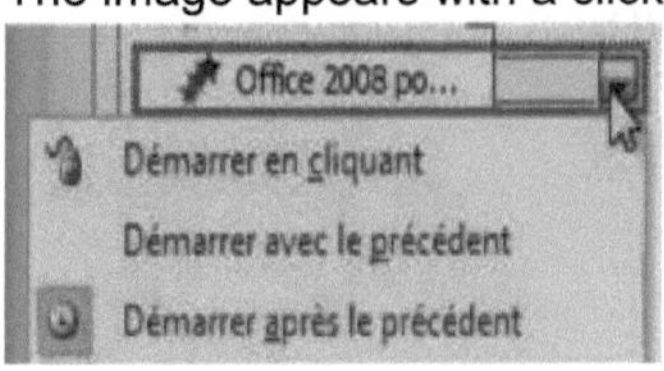

Appearance of Office 2008 text... after the previous one.

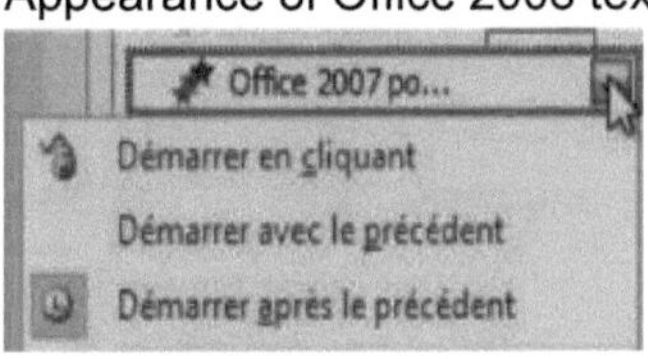

Appearance of Office 2007 text... after the previous one.

CHANGING THE ORDER OF ANIMATIONS

There are 2 ways of changing the order of the animations:

3. sliding animation.

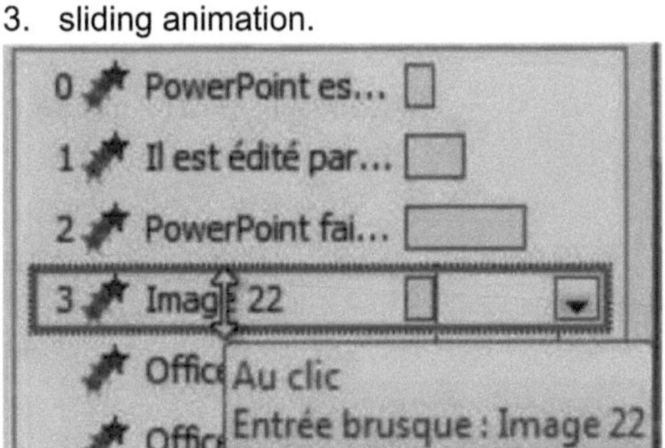

4. Select the animation you want (here 3, image 22) and a double arrow will appear.

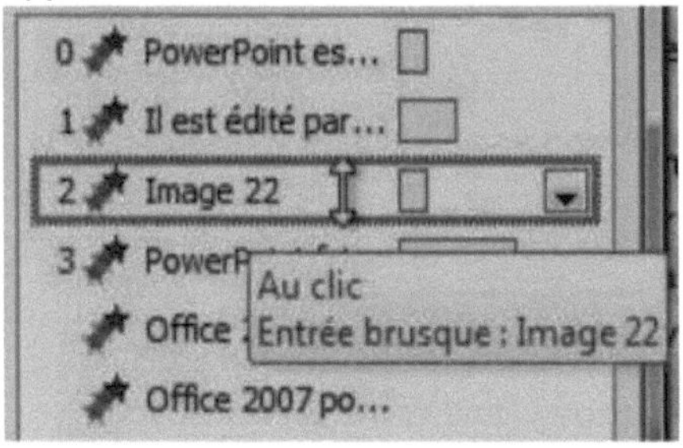

5. Move the selected animation to the desired location (here behind animation 1).
The animations are renumerated.

REORGANISING ACTIVITIES

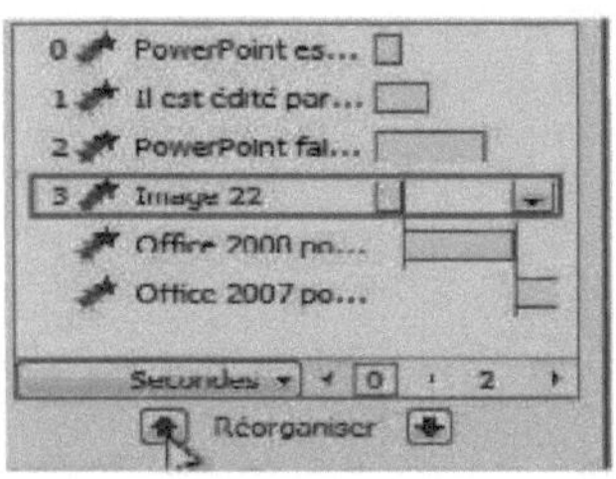

Select the animation you want (here 3, image 22), and click on the up or down

arrow at the bottom of the animations pane (Reorganise).
Move the selected animation to the required position (here behind animation 1).
The animations are renumerated.

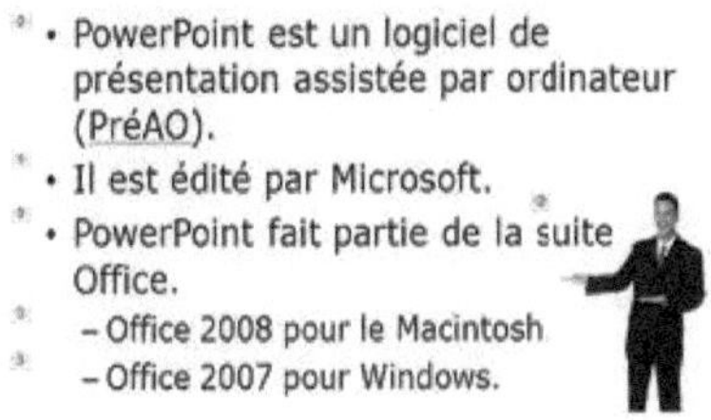

- PowerPoint is computer-assisted presentation software (PreAO).
- It is published by Microsoft.
- PowerPoint is part of the Office suite.

-Office 2008 for the Macintosh.

-Office 2007 for Windows.

Our presenter is now number 2.

Changes to effects options.

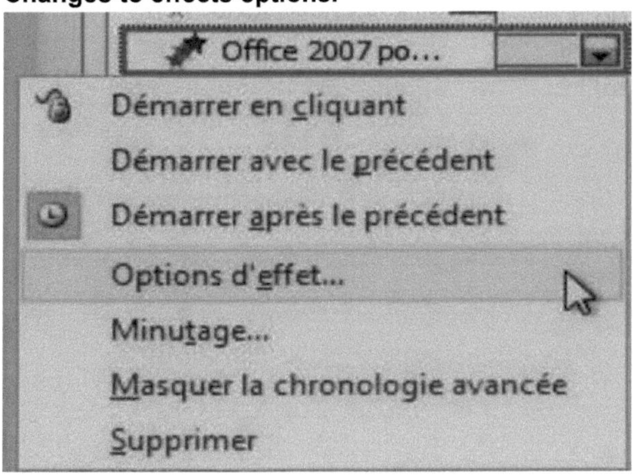

From the effect options in the animations pane, you can modify number of effect settings.

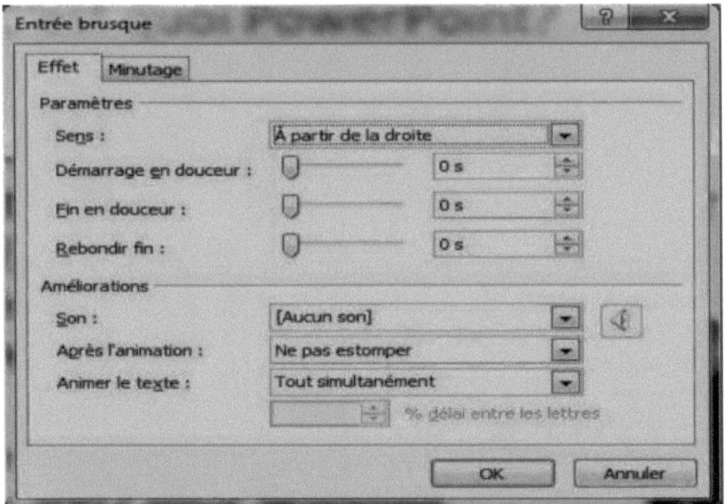

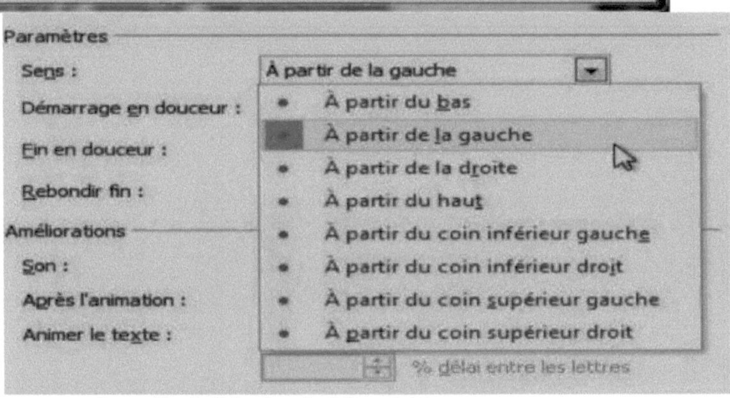

Text appears from the left instead of the right.

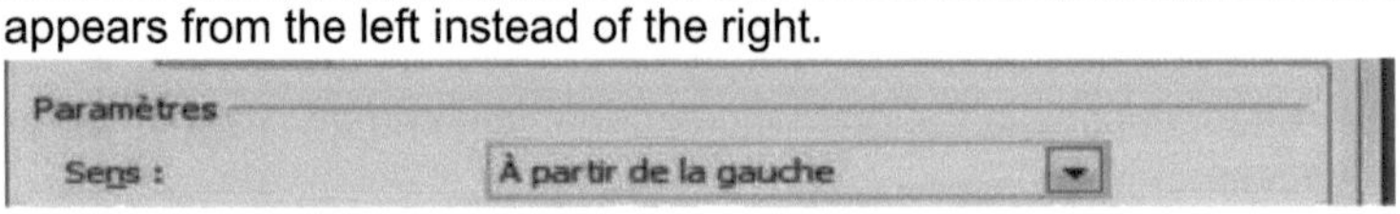

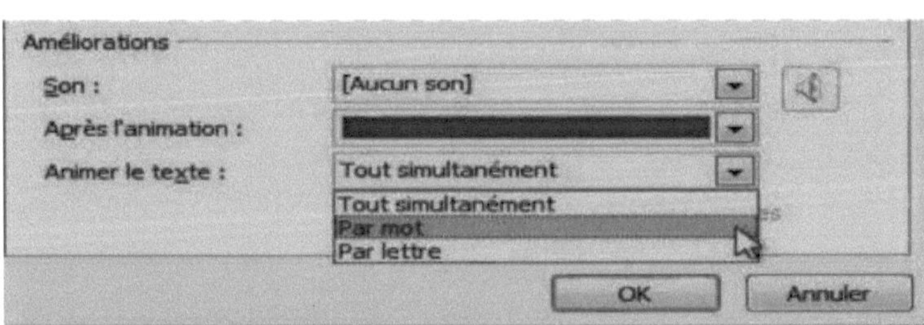

Effect after animation: the text turns blue

Other effect: display by word

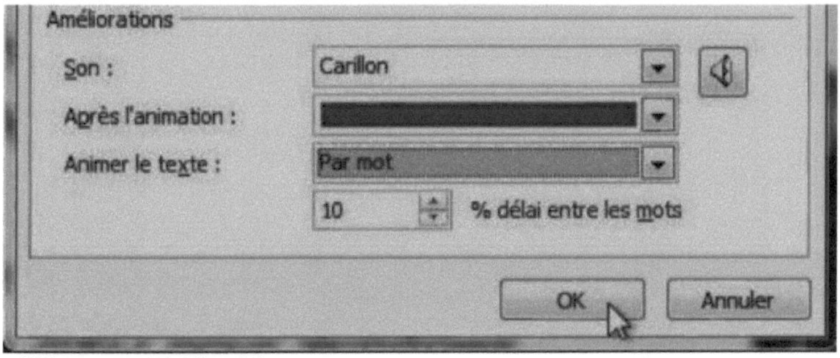

And a little sound (chimes).

VII.4.REPRODUCTION OF EVENTS

To reproduce an animation, simply follow the steps below:

7. Select the object containing the animations you wish to copy.
8. On the **Animations** tab of the toolbar ribbon, in the **Advanced Animation** group, click **Animation** .

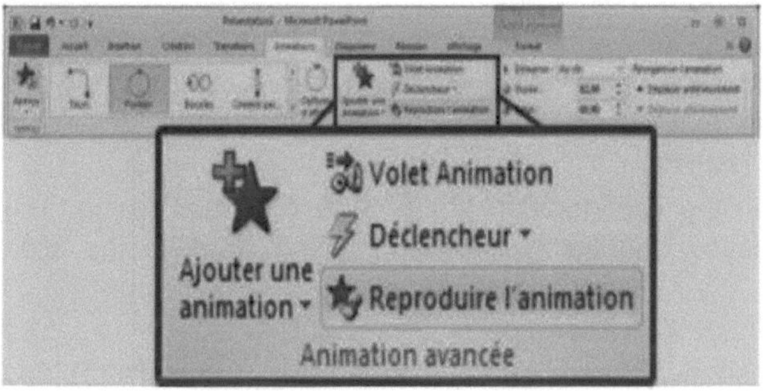

Your cursor changes to appear as follows:

9. On the slide, click on the object to which you want to copy the animations.

VII.5.TIMING

Using PowerPoint's timing feature allows you to play your presentation automatically by managing the display time of your slides. This feature will be essential for creating a presentation that needs to run in a loop on a touch terminal, for example.

TIMING YOUR SLIDES

1. Select a slide from your presentation.

2. Go to the Ribbon, Transitions tab, Timing group. Adjust the settings to launch the next slide after a set time in seconds and click Apply everywhere if you want to affect all the slides in your presentation.

Transition timing is particularly useful for automated presentations, and you can also use timing for your animations - it works in a very similar way. In this way, your slideshow can be finely timed to meet your specifications.

VII.6.CHECKING THE TIMING

In the slideshow tab, in the configuration group, click on check timing. The repeat toolbar is displayed and the presentation timing starts in the slide duration area.

Or ;

For the types of slideshow **Presented by a presenter (full screen)** and **Viewed on a terminal (full screen)**, it may be useful to check and record the timing of effects and slides.

1. In the **Slideshow** tab, click **Check timing**.

Note: The presentation timer starts as soon as you click on **Check Timing**.

The **Repeat** toolbar is displayed and the timing of the presentation begins in **the Duration** area **of the slide**.

2. Figure above: Repetition toolbar

o Next (advance to the next slide)

P Pause

и Slide length

to Repeat

и Total length of slideshow

3. While the presentation is being timed, you can perform one or more of the following operations using the **Repeat** toolbar:

- To move on to the next slide, click **Next.**
- To stop recording temporarily, click on **Suspend**.
- resume recording for the duration of the pause, click **Pause**.

- To set the exact display time for a slide, enter the corresponding value in the **Slide time** field.
- resume recording for the duration of the active slide, click **Repeat**.

4. Once the duration of the last slide has been set, a message displays the total duration of the presentation and prompts you to perform one of the following operations:

- To keep the timings of the recorded slides, click **Yes.**
- To remove the timings from the saved slides, click **No.** Slide sorter mode is activated and displays the duration of each slide in your presentation.

CHAPTER VIII

IMAGES WITH POWERPOINT

Imagery is also simply defined as a set of images with either the same origin and a defined style (e.g. Epinal imagery), or the same style and genre (e.g. popular imagery). School imagery, which is limited to the school environment, is another example.[6]

VIII.1.INSERTING AN IMAGE

Depending on the version of PowerPoint you are using, you can insert images, photos or clipart into your slideshow from your computer or from the Internet.

1. Click where you wish to insert the image on the slide.
2. Under the **Insert** tab, go to the **Images** group, click on **Images,** then on **This device**.

3. In the dialogue box that opens, find the image you want to insert, select it, then click **Insert**.

Tip: To insert several images simultaneously, select them by holding down the Ctrl key.

INSERTING IMAGES STORED ON A SLIDE

1. Click where you wish to insert the image on the slide.
2. In the **Insert** tab, go to the **Images** group, click on **Images** , then on **Stored images**.

3. Type a description of the image you are looking for, click on the images you want and then click **Insert**.

[6] https://www.techno-science.net, consulted on 19/10/2023 at 14h18'

INSERT AN IMAGE FROM THE WEB ON YOUR SLIDE

1. Click where you wish to insert the image on the slide.
2. Under the **Insert** tab, go to the **Images** group, click on **Images**, then on **Online images**.

NB:

- If the message "the service required to use this feature is disabled" is displayed, you need to check your confidentiality settings. To do this, **go to File**> **Account**> **Account confidentiality** then click on **Manage settings**. Tick the box **Enable optional connected experiences**, click OK, then restart PowerPoint.
- Contact your administrator if you do not have access to the confidentiality settings.

3. In the search box, type a description of the image you are looking for, then press enter.
4. Select the images you want, then click **Insert**.

Tip: After inserting an image, you can change its size and position. To do this, right-click on the image, then click **Image Shaper**. You can then use **the Image Shaping** tools on the right of your slide.

INSERT AN IMAGE IN THE SLIDE MASK

If you want an image to appear on all the slides of a specific type in your PowerPoint template, add it to the slide mask.

INSERT AN IMAGE IN THE BACKGROUND

If you want an image to appear in the background without affecting all the slides in a mask, change background settings on the slide.

VIII.2.RESIZING AN IMAGE

CROPPING AN IMAGE IN POWERPOINT

Once the first point has been validated, you can then adapt the contours of an image by cropping it to the chosen shape. The visual will then be automatically cut to fill the geometry of the selected shape, while retaining its original proportions.

To do this, **follow these simple steps**:

1. Insert the image on a slide in your PowerPoint presentation

2. Click on the image to open the lie menu in the top bar
3. Select the "Crop" tab, then "Crop to shape".
4. Choose the shape you want to crop

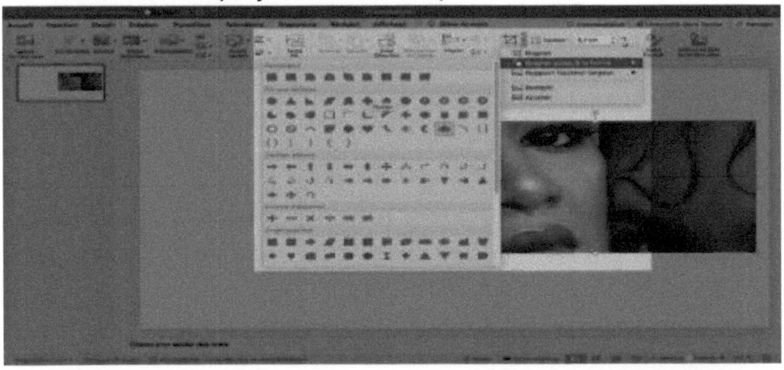

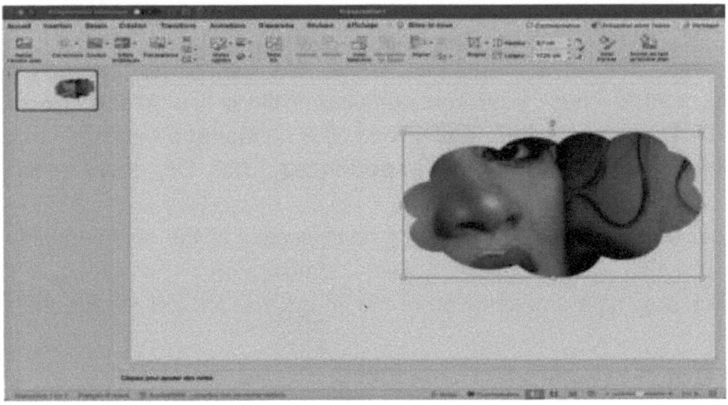

The shape is then automatically applied to the image. You can also **adjust the position of the shape within the frame** by dragging it inside the frame, for example to centre the most important part of the image. Finally, don't forget to caption the image, or at least add a comment, to give it a context for your future presentation.

Good to know

If you want to crop the same image into several shapes, make as many copies of the visual and crop each one individually.

RESIZE THE IMAGE IN THE FORM

Finally, you can adjust the image if it is tilted, truncated or does not fill the shape as you wish. To do this, go back to the 'Format image' menu, then to the 'Crop' tab. Clicking on the arrow under the 'Crop' tab brings up a menu displaying the various options for cropping.

You have two options:

- **Fill**: the shape is inserted within the limits of the image, and the parts outside are removed

- **Fit**: as much of the image as possible is adapted to the shape. The original proportions of the image are retained, which may result in an empty space inside the shape.

You can also adjust the size of the solid shape using the **resizing handles**: position the pointer over one of the points, then click and drag as required.

When you have finished, press the Esc key or click anywhere on the document, then save your changes if you are happy with them.

CHAPTER IX

FLOWCHARTS WITH POWERPOINT

An organisation chart gives you a schematic presentation of the hierarchical, organisational or functional links within your structure.

1. Graph of the structure of a complex organisation (company, group, etc.), representing both the various elements of the group and their respective relationships .[7]
2. In computing, graphical representation of a problem, its analysis and resolution using symbols to express operations, data, links or devices .[8]

IX.1.INSERTING AN ORGANISATION CHART

Although PowerPoint is an incomparable tool for generating presentations, its diagram creation functionality is extremely limited. You can see this for yourself in the following sections. Follow the instructions below to create your flowchart in PowerPoint.

1. INSERTING A SMARTART ELEMENT

In your PowerPoint document, go to the Insert tab and click on SmartArt. Once you have clicked on the SmartArt button, go to the Hierarchy group in the left-hand column and select the flowchart model that suits your needs.

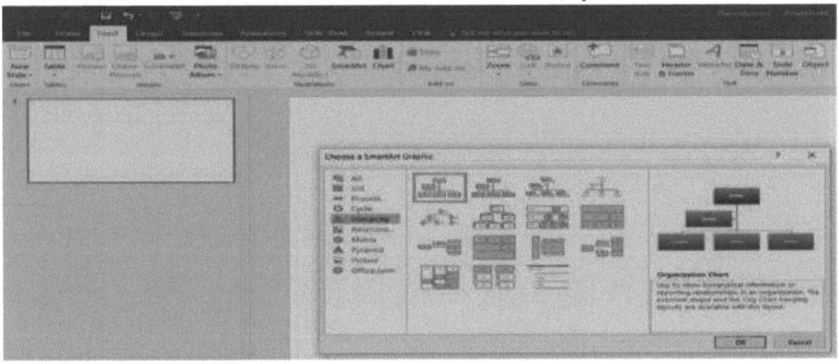

2. ENTER YOUR TEXT

Now click on one of the shapes to add your text. As each shape represents a person in the company, you need to check that everyone is included in the diagram.

---

[7] https://www.larousse.fr, consulted on 19/10/2023 at 15:09'.
[8] Ditto

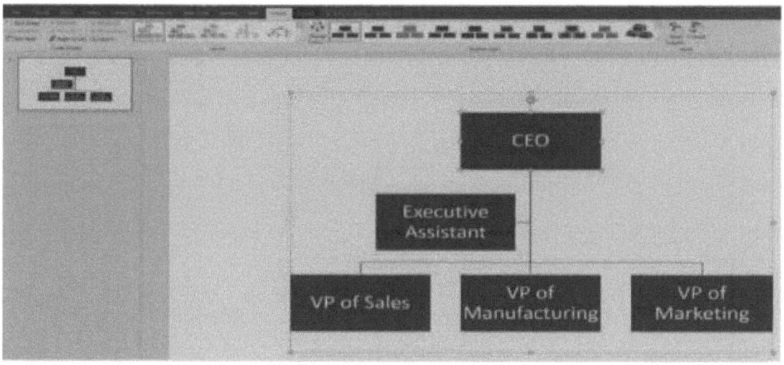

3. ADD SHAPES.

It is likely that you will not find the exact shape you need to represent your company in the models proposed by SmartArt. In this case, you will need to add additional shapes. To do this, click on the Creation tab in the SmartArt Tools section, then click on the Add a shape button. In the menu which appears, you can choose where the person should be placed in the organisation chart, who their hierarchical superior is, and who their subordinates are.
Let's imagine that your company has recruited a vice-president of human resources who reports to the CEO, a sales representative who reports to the vice-president of sales. These relationships can be modelled in the Creation tab of the SmartArt Tools section using the Add Shape button.

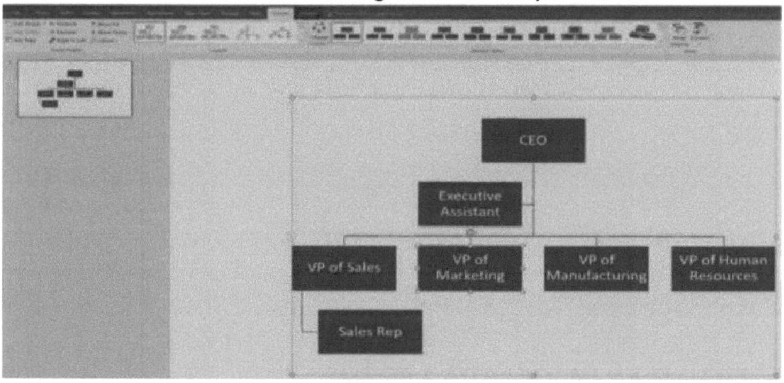

4. CUSTOMISING THE HIERARCHY

To rearrange the layout of your flowchart in PowerPoint, first click on the shape you want to move. Then, from the Creation tab in the SmartArt Tools section, you can move this shape vertically using the Move Up or Move Down buttons, or horizontally using the Move Up or Move Down buttons.
Let's imagine that while you're creating your organisation chart in PowerPoint, the structure of your company changes and the Vice President of Marketing now reports to the Vice President of Sales. To reflect this change, click on the

Vice of Marketing, then on the Collapse button in the Creation tab.

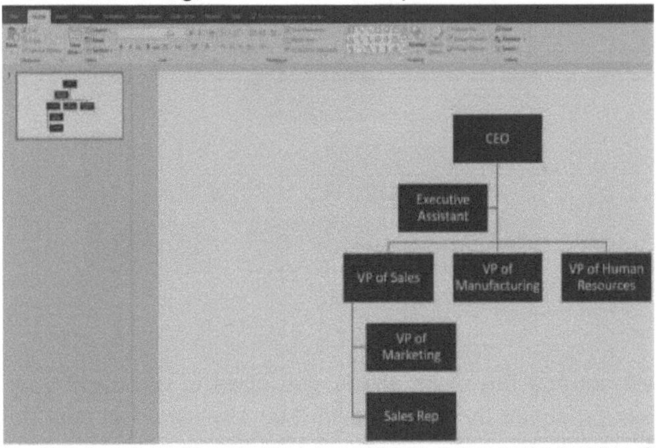

5. SHAPING THE DESIGN OF YOUR ORGANISATION CHART

Once you've optimised the layout of your flowchart in PowerPoint, you can move on to improving its appearance. Using the fonts, colours and layout styles you'll find at the top of your screen, improve your flowchart to make it both intuitive and informative.

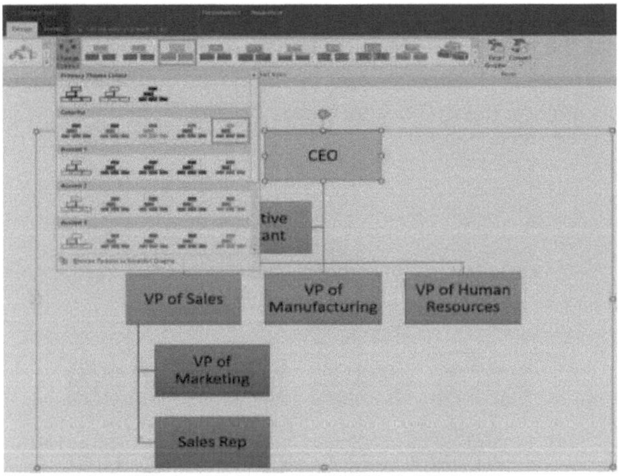

IX.2.INSERTING AN IMAGE INTO A FRAME

1. Click on the shape to which you want to add an image.
2. On the **Format** tab, in the **Shape styles** group, click on the arrow next to **Shape fill**.

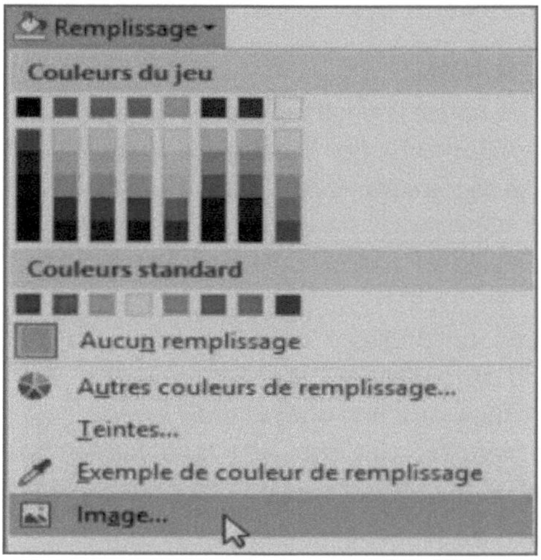

3. In folder or location containing the image you want to use, click on the image file, then on **Insert**.

Note: You cannot change the position of the image within the shape.

CHAPTER X

OBJECTS DRAWINGS POWERPOINT

As in all Microsoft Office programs, an object is anything that the program can manipulate (move, display, etc.) but not modify. For example, a photo is seen as an object in Word and Excel: these two programs can display it, size it, print it, etc., but not modify its content. Objects in Powerpoint include images, clipart, tables, etc. Each object will be viewed in detail on a future page.

X.1.INSERT A RECTANGLE

You can add shapes, such as squares, rectangles, circles and arrows, to your documents, emails, slideshows and spreadsheets. To add a shape, click **Insert**, click **Shapes**, select a shape, then click and drag to draw it.

Once you've added one or more shapes, you can add text, bullets and numbers to them. You can also change the fill, outline and other effects in the **Format** tab.

NB: You can add individual shapes to a graph or add shapes above a SmartArt Graph to customise the graph or chart.

Adding a form in Excel, Outlook, Word or PowerPoint

1. On the **Insert** tab, click **Shapes**.

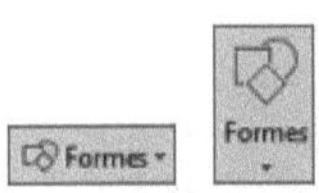

2. Click on the desired shape, then anywhere in the workspace, and drag the mouse to delimit the shape.

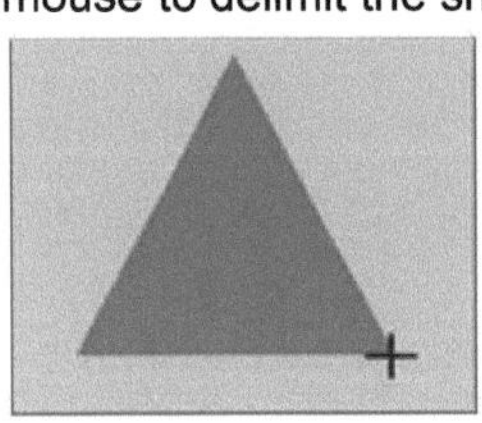

To create a perfect square or circle (or constrain the dimensions of other shapes), hold down the Shift key while dragging the mouse.

X.2.RESIZING SHAPES

To change the dimensions of a shape by dragging ;

1. Select the shape you want to resize.
2. Click and drag one of the selection handles which appear on the dimensions or at the corners.

To maintain the proportions of the shape, drag a corner handle, or hold down the Shift key and drag the handle. Visio The width and height of the selected shape appear in the status bar at the bottom of the window.

To change the dimensions of a shape by entering measurements

1. On the **View** tab, in the **View** group, click **Blob panes**, then **Size and**

position.

2. Select the shape you wish to resize.
3. Enter the width and height of the shape.

Press Enter or click on another value to validate the new value.

X.3.ALIGNING DRAWING OBJECTS

The **automatic shapes, images, graphics** and **text blocks** you add can be aligned, grouped, sorted and distributed horizontally and vertically on a slide in **the presentation editor**. To perform one of these actions, first select one or more objects in the work area. To select several objects, hold down the **Ctrl** key and left-click on the required objects. To select a block of text, click on its edge, not on the text inside. You can then use either the icons in the top toolbar described below or similar options in the context menu.

ALIGN OBJECTS

To **align** *two or more* selected objects,

1. Click on the **Align a shape** icon in the **Home** tab the top toolbar and select one of the available options:

- **Align to slide** to align objects with the edges of the slide,
- **Align selected objects** (this option is selected by default) to align objects in relation to each other,

2. Click again on the **Align shape** icon and select the type of alignment required from the list:

- **Align left**: to align objects horizontally to the left side of the leftmost object/the left edge of the slide,
- **Align to centre**: to align objects horizontally to the centre of the slide,
- **Align right**: to align objects horizontally to the right-hand side of the right-most object/right edge of the slide,
- **Align to top**: to align objects vertically to the top edge of the highest object/the top edge of the slide,
- **Align to centre**: to align objects vertically by their centre/middle of the slide,
- **Align at bottom**: to align objects vertically by the bottom edge of the lowest object/bottom edge of the slide.

You can also right-click on the selected objects, choose **Align** from the context menu, then use one of the available alignment options.

If you want to align a single object, it can be aligned relative to the edges of the slide. The **Align to slide** option is selected by default in this case.

DISTRIBUTE OBJECTS

To **distribute** *three or more selected objects* horizontally or vertically so that the same distance appears between them,

1. Click on the **Align** icon in the **Home** tab the top toolbar and select one of the available options:

- **Align on slide** to distribute objects between the edges of the slide,

- **Align selected objects** (this option is selected by default) to distribute the objects between the two outermost objects selected,

2. Click on the **Align shape** icon again and select the required distribution type from the list:

- **Distribute horizontally**: to distribute the objects evenly between the left and right edges of the selected objects and the left and right edges of the slide.
- **Distribute vertically**: to distribute objects evenly between the top and bottom edges of the selected objects and the top and bottom edges of the slide...

You can also right-click on the selected objects, choose **Align** from the context menu, then use one of the available distribution options.

Note: the distribution options are disabled if you select fewer than three objects.

ORGANISE SEVERAL OBJECTS

To **organise** the selected objects (i.e. to change their order when several objects overlap), click on the **Organise Shape** icon in the **Home** tab the top toolbar and select the required type from the list.

- **Move to foreground**: to move objects in front of all other objects,
- **Move one level forward**: to move objects one level forward in relation to other objects.
- **Move to background**: to move objects behind all other objects,
- **Move back one level**: to move objects one level backwards in relation to other objects.

You can also right-click on the selected objects, choose **Organise** from the context menu, and then use one of the available storage options.

X .4.GROUP DRAWING OBJECTS

To **group** or **ungroup** *two or more* selected objects, click the **Organise Shape** icon on the **Home** tab the top toolbar and select the required option from the list:

- **Group**: to combine several objects so that you can rotate, move, resize, align, organise, copy, paste and format them simultaneously as a single object.
- **Unlink**: to unlink the selected group previously combined objects.

You can also right-click on the selected objects, choose the **Order** option from the context menu, then use the **Group** or **Ungroup** option.

Note: the **Group** option is disabled if fewer than two objects are selected. The **Ungroup** option is only available when a group of previously joined objects is selected.

CHAPTER XI

POWERPOINT VIDEOS

Add videos to your slides to enhance your PowerPoint presentations! Microsoft's software has all the functions you need for cropping, trimming, colouring, full-screen playback and automatic start-up.

XI .1.INSERT A VIDEO

You can choose to integrate a clip stored on your computer or a YouTube video that will be played on the fly, in streaming mode, which requires an Internet connection. Note, however, that YouTube clips will not benefit from the special effects.

- In PowerPoint, position yourself on the slide that is to receive the video.
- Under the **Insert** tab, click on **Video** and select the clip on your computer (**This device**), or download free videos offered by Microsoft (**Store videos**) or enter the address of a clip posted on a video-sharing site such as YouTube or Vimeo (**Online videos**).

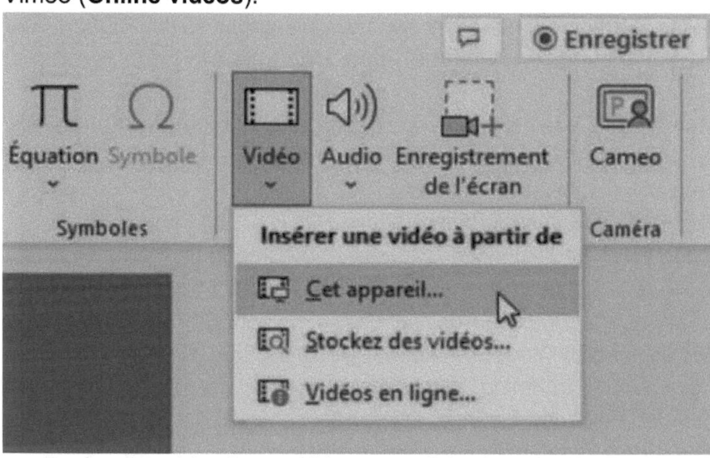

- Resize the video by grabbing one of the handles at the four corners of the video (avoid grabbing the other handles as this will distort the image).

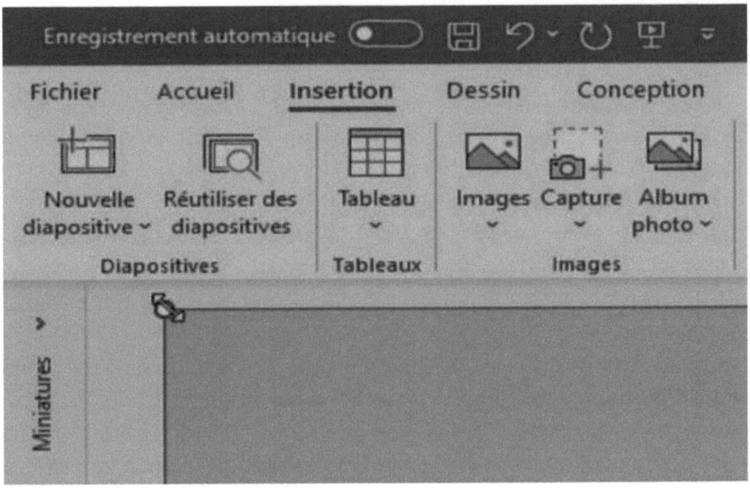

- When a video is selected in a slide, two tabs are added to the Ribbon. The **Video Format** tab is used to format the video, colour it, apply effects, crop it, etc.
- The **Playback** tab is used to set various parameters, such as automatically launching the video, cutting it out to keep only an extract, playing it in a loop while the slide is still displayed, and so on.

TRIMMING A VIDEO IN POWERPOINT

Cropping a video involves displaying only part of the image, in height or width, instead of the full rectangular frame. Once the main subject has been cropped, you can even apply effects (round or star shape, colouring...). In PowerPoint, cropping is not allowed on YouTube videos. Don't confuse "cropping a video" with "trimming a video": trimming means, for example, keeping a 10-second extract from a video that lasts 1 minute.

- Click on **the video** to select it.
- Click on **Format video > Crop**.
- Position the mouse pointer next a black crop handle,

grab it and slide it over.

- Click the **Crop** button again to confirm, or press **Esc** to cancel.

- The operation is not definitive, and you can use the **Crop** function again to reduce or re-expand the area to be displayed.
- The cropping options are visible in the vertical pane by right-clicking on the video and choosing **Video format**.

- To reset all the effects applied to a video, click on **Video format > Restore original presentation.**
- To reset all the effects applied to a video with a single click, **click Video format > Restore original presentation.**

XI.2.PLAY/START VIDEO

First and foremost, the video must start as soon as its slide is displayed. This can be a video embedded in the PowerPoint file or an external video, such as a "linked" video stored on your hard disk or a YouTube video. Note that if your slide has animation steps beforehand, these steps will run before the video clip starts.

- Click on the video to select it.
- Under the **Playback**, click on **Start: Automatically**.

Play a video only if you click on it

Please note that the video will only launch if you click within its frame. Clicking anywhere else on the slide (or pressing the Space bar, for example) will not launch the clip.

- Click on the video to select it.
- In the **Playback** tab, click **Start: On click**.

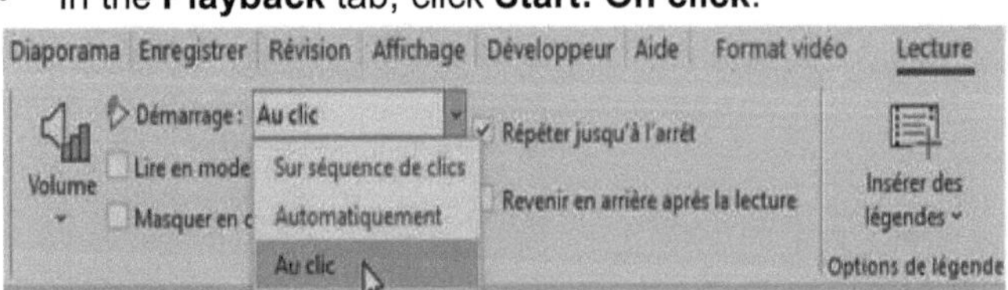

LAUNCH A VIDEO WHEN YOU CLICK ON THE SLIDE

When the slide is displayed, the video should not start. It will start when the mouse is next clicked on the slide, depending on the timing of the animations you have defined for this slide. This option was introduced with PowerPoint 2016.

- Click on the video to select it.
- In the **Playback** tab, click **Start: On sequence of clicks** on PC, or **Start: On click in sequence** on Mac.

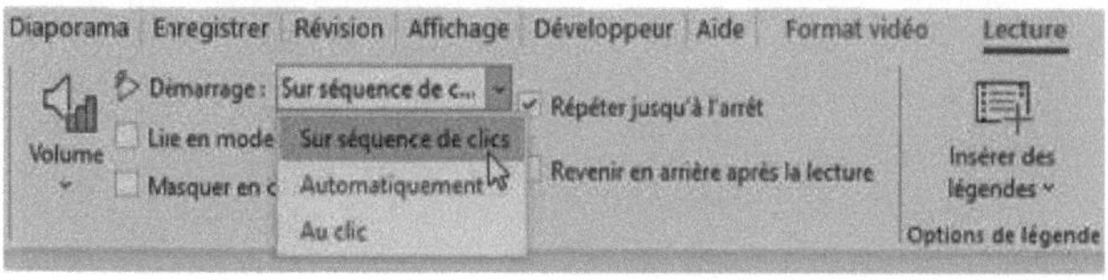

- If you want to specify the timing of animations and video playback for a slide, add triggers, etc., click **on the Animations** tab **> Animation pane.**

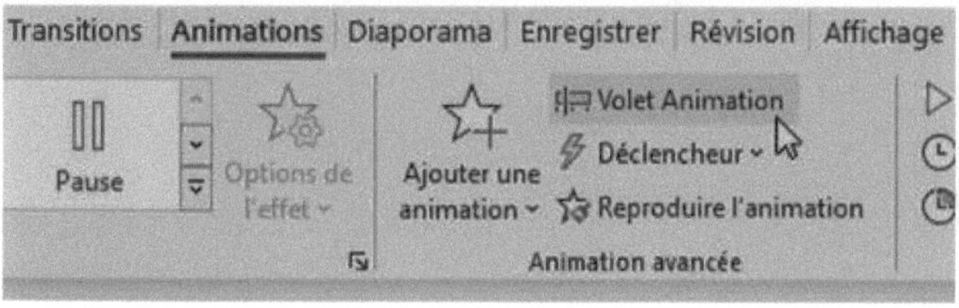

ý In the *Animation pane*, rearrange the elements and add animations and triggers.

IX.3.EMPTY RIBBON

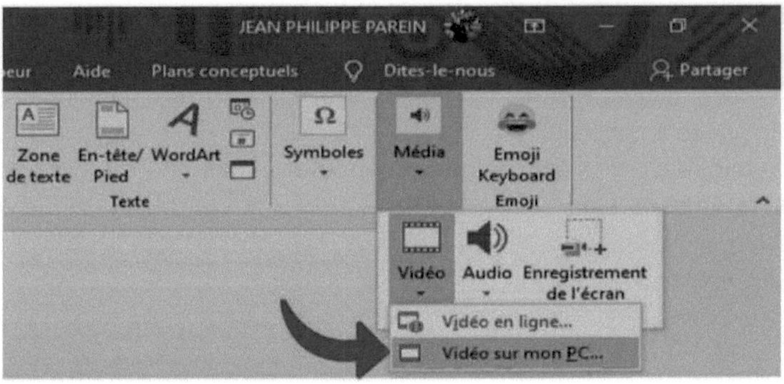
JEAN PHILIPPE PAREIN
Aide
Plans conceptuels
Dites-le-nous
Partager
Zone de texte
En-tête/ Pied
WordArt
Texte
Symboles
Média
Emoji Keyboard
Emoji
Vidéo
Audio
Enregistrement de l'écran
Vidéo en ligne...
Vidéo sur mon PC...

CHAPTER XII

POWERPOINT PHOTO

XII.1.CREATING A PHOTO ALBUM

To create a **Photo Album**, proceed as follows:

1. On the **Insert** tab, in the **Images** group, click the **Photo album** button :

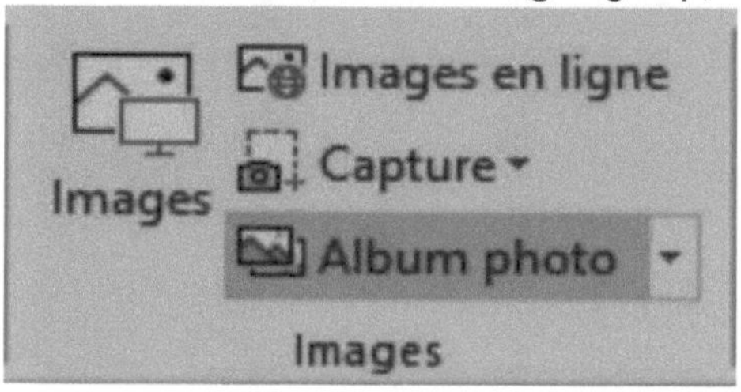

Or select the **Photo album** drop-down list and click on **New photo album...** :

2. In the **Photo Album** dialog box :

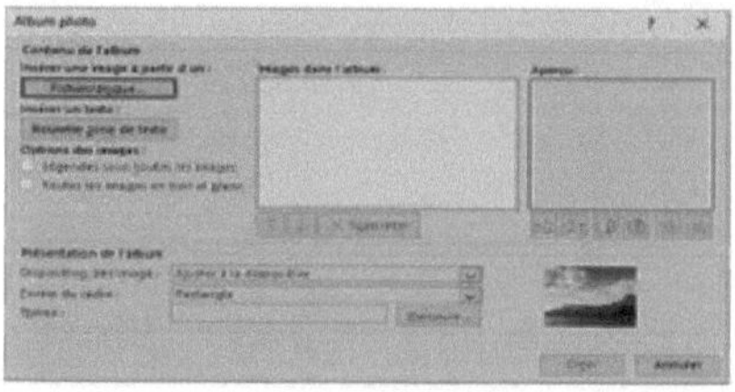

2.1. Click on the **File/Disc...** button to select the images you want to insert:

- To select several images, hold down the **Ctrl** or **Shift** key while clicking on the ones you want.
- To select all the images in the folder, **click Ctrl+A**.

2.2. For each image in the **Images in album** list, select the image, then apply the necessary corrections using the buttons below the **Preview** pane:

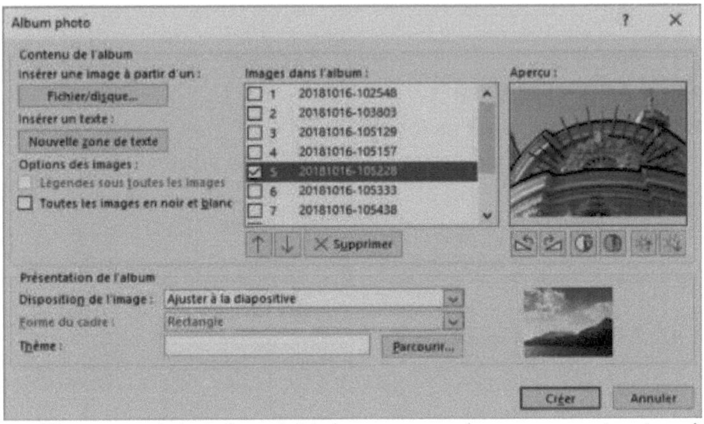

- You can rotate left or right, increase or decrease contrast and increase or decrease brightness.
- Use the arrows to move an image up or down

in order.

2.3. In the **Album Layout** section, open the **Image Layout** drop-down list and choose the layout you prefer.
prefer :

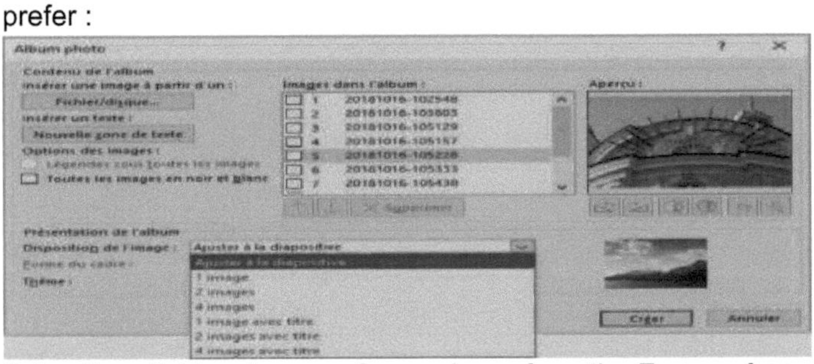

2.4. If available, choose a frame shape from the **Frame shape** list. Some of the choices in the previous step do not allow you to choose a frame shape:

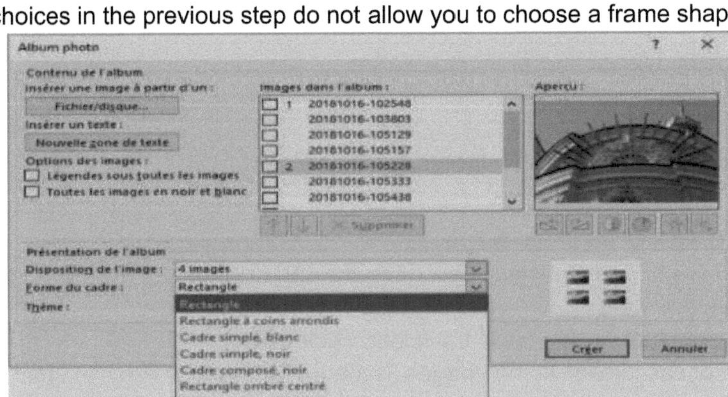

2.5. You can create themes specifically for albums

and then use them here by clicking on the **Browse...** button to search for a theme. You may also want to experiment with the photo album themes in the dialog box when you create your photo album.
initially the photo album.

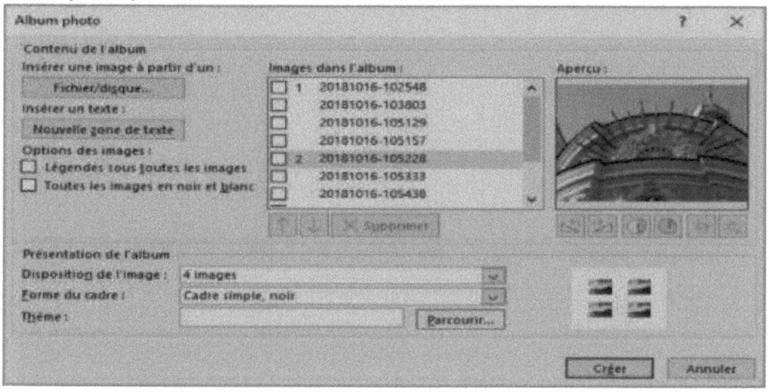

2.6. To add caption areas to each image, tick the **Captions** box **under all images.**

2.7. To display images in black and white, tick the **All black and white images** box.

3. Click on the **Create** button.

XII.2.INSERTING A SOUND

A) ADD AUDIO FROM A LOCAL FILE

Step 1. Open the PowerPoint presentation

Open the PowerPoint presentation and click on "Insert" > "Insert".
Audio". Then select "Audio on my PC".

Step 2. Insert the sound

The file explorer tab opens, and you can locate the sound file you want to use, then click on "Insert".

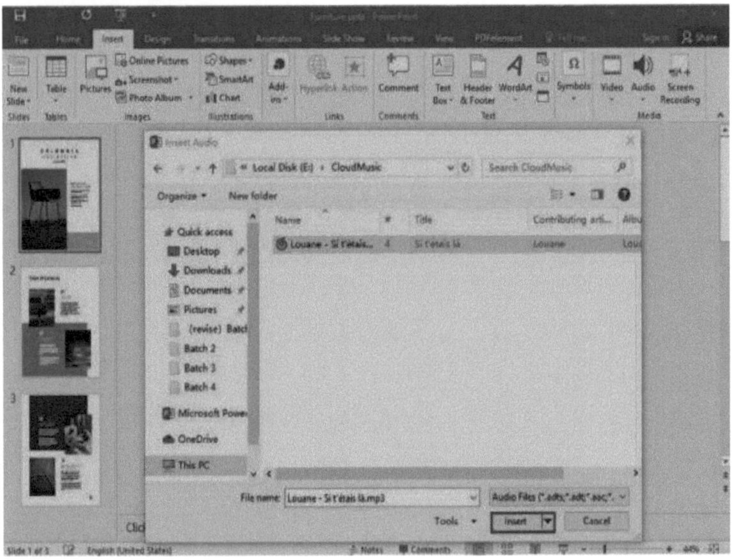

B) ADD AN AUDIO RECORDING

Step 1. Open the slide

First you need to open the slide where you want to add the audio, and you can click on "Insert" > "Audio". Then you can choose the 'Record audio' option.

Step 2. Record the audio

Once you have opened the recording option, you can change the name of your audio recording. Then click on the "Record" button to start the audio. Once it has finished, stop the recording. Then click on "OK".

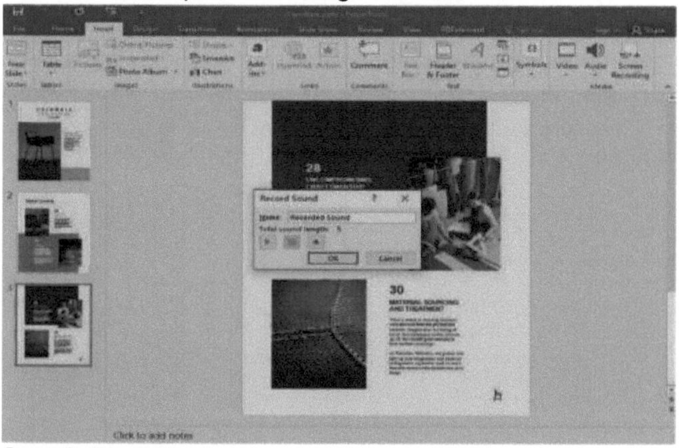

Step 3. Play the audio

Now you can select the "Play" button to check the audio. You can also select the "Play" option.

Reading in the background" to make the presentation more attractive.

XII.3.EDITING A PHOTO ALBUM

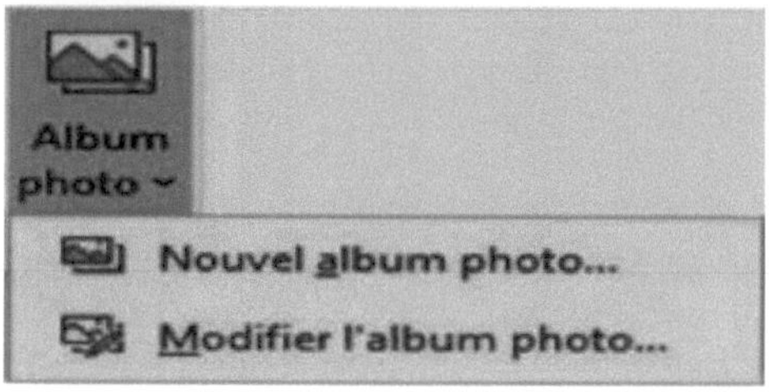

To modify the photo album, i.e. modify all the photos rather than just one photo at a time, go to the **'Insert'** tab, **'Photo album'** control and then click on

'Modify photo album ...'; the 'Photo album' window reappears. Make your changes, then click **'Update'.** All the changes authorised when the album was created are possible including adding new photos.

Please note that when modifications are made, the photo album is recreated; consequently, modifications made previously and individually to one or more slides will disappear. Only the adjustments made in the 'Photo Album' window will be taken into account.

CHAPTER XIII

USE OF SCANNER

A scanner is a computer peripheral, like a printer, connected to a computer. It enables the user to digitise a paper document into a digital image that appears on the computer screen. The paper passes under a light beam which captures the information contained on the document and retranscribes it. Once digitised, the document can be modified or saved directly on the computer. There are several types of scanner.

> The flatbed scanner: the document is placed on a glass surface and a beam of light scans the page and transmits the information to the computer.

> The hand-held scanner: the document is placed on a flat surface and the user uses this device to move it over the paper.

> Scroll scanner: similar to a fax machine. The document is scanned in front of a fixed light slot which digitises the content of the paper.[9]

XIII.1.INSTALLATION

The scanning principle is based on the scanning of the surface of a document, placed on the glass a printer or scanner, by a moving lamp located at its extremities. The lamp diffuses light which is reflected line by line by a set of mirrors. The light rays are converged towards a sensor to be reconstructed. Using a USB connection, the image is transferred to a computer.

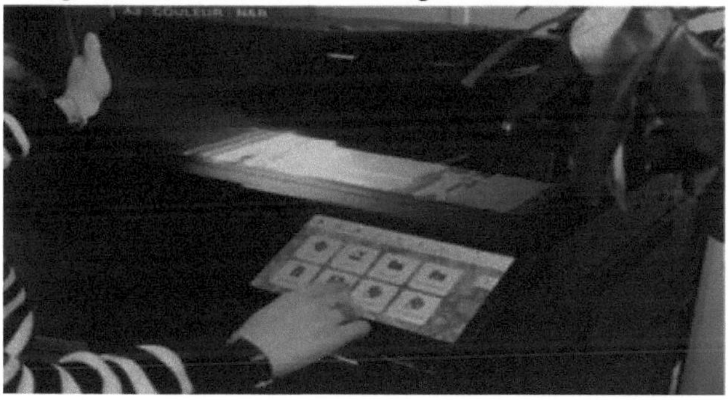

To use a scanner, first install it, then insert the installation CD into your computer's CD drive, if there is no CD. Then visit the manufacturer's website to download installation files and follow the installation instructions.

FOR USB SCANNERS

Simply follow the instructions below:

- exit and terminate all programs on the computer without shutting it down;
- connect the USB scanner to the computer ;
- connect the scanner's power supply ;
- switch on the scanner and wait until the PC recognises the installed device

[9] https: //www.location-entretien-photocopieur. fr, consulted on 20/10/2023 at 06h23'

- appearance of the scanner hardware manager on the computer.

FOR FIREWIRE SCANNERS

Follow the steps below:

- exit and terminate all programs on the computer without shutting it down;
- connect the scanner to a FireWire port on the computer;
- power the scanner ;
- turn on the scanner and wait for the driver to be identified;
- follow the instructions displayed by the equipment manager.

FOR THE SCSI SCANNER

Follow the steps below:

- insert the SCSI card and connect it to the PC bus connector ;
- replace the cover and tighten the case;
- insert the SCSI card and connect it to the PC bus connector ;
- connect the parallel connector to the printer port ;
- connecting and powering the epiniere scanner ;
- switch on the scanner and computer ;
- follow the instructions displayed by the equipment manager.

XIII.2.USE

1. Launch the utility, then search for a **Numeriser** button or menu. In our example, it's called **Num/Import**.

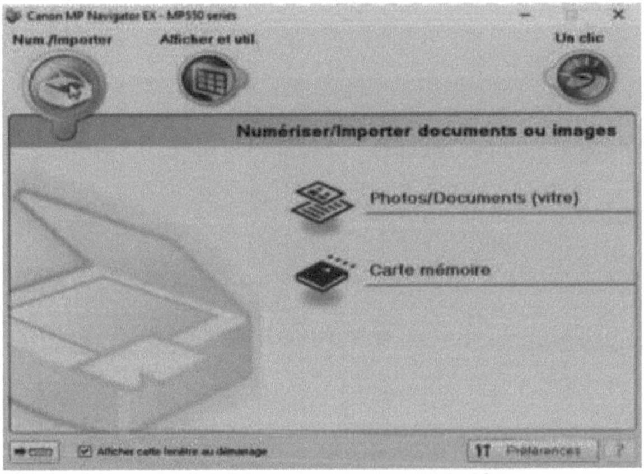

2. If the software offers it, activate the **Use scanner driver** option.

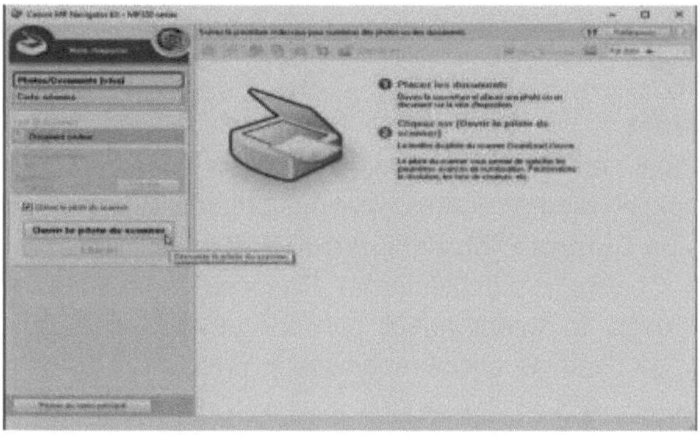

3. Your machine is now detected and ready to use. Click on the **Aperqu** or **Preview** button to check that everything is working correctly.

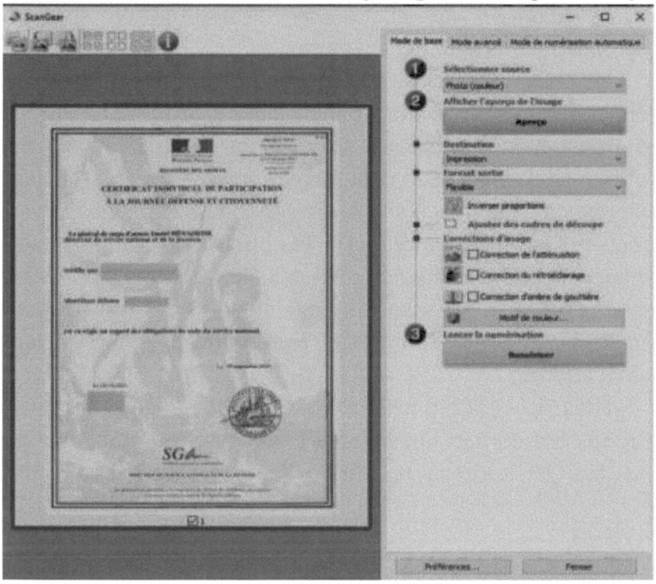

CHAPTER XIV

INTERNET NETWORK

Definition of Reseau internet:

A set of interconnected global networks that enable computers and servers to communicate efficiently using a common communications protocol (IP) .[10]

XIV.1 TCP/IP (Transmission Control Protocol/Internet Protocol)

TCP/IP, or Transmission Control Protocol/Internet Protocol, is a suite of communication protocols used to interconnect network devices over the Internet. TCP/IP can also be used as a communications protocol in a local area network (LAN).

The entire suite of Internet protocols, i.e. a set of rules and procedures, is commonly referred to as TCP/IP, although others are included in the suite. The TCP/IP protocol suite acts as an abstraction layer between Internet applications and the routing and switching structure.

The TCP/IP protocol specifies how data is exchanged over the Internet by providing end-to-end communications that identify how it is to be split into packets, addressed, transmitted, routed and resent at the destination. TCP/IP requires little central management and is designed to make networks reliable, with the ability to automatically recover if any device on the network fails.

The two main protocols in the Internet protocol suite perform specific functions.

> **TCP** defines how applications can create communication channels across a network. It also manages how a message is assembled into small packets before being transmitted over the internet and reassembled in the correct order at the destination address.

> **The IP address** defines how each packet should be addressed and routed to ensure that it reaches the correct destination. Each gateway computer on the network checks this IP address to determine where to forward the message.

TCP/IP MODEL LAYERS

TCP/IP functionality is divided into four layers, each of which contains specific protocols:

- **The application layer** provides applications with a standardised data exchange. Its protocols include HTTP, FTP, HTTP, etc.
- Post Office Protocol 3 (POP3), Simple Mail Transfer Protocol (SMTP) and Simple Network Management Protocol (SNMP). At the application layer, the payload is the actual data from the application.
- **The transport layer** is responsible for maintaining end-to-end communications on the network. The TCP protocol manages communications between hosts and provides flow control, multiplexing and reliability. Transport protocols include TCP and User Data Protocol (UDP), which is sometimes

[10] https://actualiteinformatique.fr, consulted on 20/10/2023 at 06:49'.

used in place of TCP for special purposes.

- **The network layer**, also known as the internet layer, processes packets and connects independent networks to transport packets across network boundaries. The network layer protocols are IP and ICMP (Internet Control Message Protocol), which is used for error notification.
- **The physical layer,** also known as the network interface layer or data link layer, is made up of protocols that only work on a link, i.e. the network element that interconnects the nodes or hosts in the network. Protocols at this lower layer include Ethernet for Local Area Networks (LANs) and Address Resolution Protocol (ARP).

XIV.2.LOCAL NETWORK SHARING

NETWORKING PCS

Microsoft has greatly simplified the operations required to link several PCs to a local network. Each will be able to access a folder provided by a user on their own computer. Obviously, for everything to work perfectly, each machine must be connected to the Internet box via Ethernet or Wi-Fi.

> To begin with, you need to check that each PC that is to join the network is using the same configuration as the Internet box. By default, Windows 10 considers your box's network to be a public network and applies certain restrictions. Go to Windows *Settings* by pressing the **Win+** I keys on your keyboard, then click on **Network and Internet**.

> The *Status* window that appears shows how your computer is connected to the Internet (in this case, via the Wi-Fi network set up by the box). Click on the **Properties** button located on the type of connection used.

> In the *Network Profile* section, activate the **Private** box if you haven't already done so. This will give you access to file and printer sharing. Repeat these operations on each PC.

> Now return to the previous window by clicking on the **arrow at the top left of** the interface, next to *Settings*. Scroll down and click on the **Networking and Sharing Centre** link.

> The Windows Control Panel is displayed with the settings options. In the left-hand pane, click on the **Modify advanced sharing settings** link.

> In the *Private (current)* section, check that **the Enable network discovery** box is ticked, as is the **Enable automatic configuration of devices connected to the network** box.

> Now unroll the *All networks* section. In the *Public folder sharing* section, tick the **Enable sharing (...)** box to open access to the user's *Public* folder. In the *Password-protected sharing* section, tick the **Disable password-protected sharing** box. Without this precaution, each member of the household would have to have a user account on this PC to share files. Click the **Save Changes** button at the bottom of the window. Repeat these operations on all the PCs that are to join the network.

> Your PCs now have the right configuration for sharing files. On one of them, open File Explorer by pressing the **Win+** E keys on the keyboard. Click on **the arrow** to the left of *Quick Access* and choose **Network**.

> Windows Explorer shows all the machines currently connected to your local network. The computers you have just configured (including the one you are using), but also your box, if it can act as a server;

> Double-click **on the name of one of the** connected **PCs**. In the window that appears, enter a user name: you can type anything, even a word that doesn't match any name. Do not enter a password in the next field and click **OK**.

> File Explorer displays a *Users* folder icon. Open it. You will now see a *Public* folder. You can drop any file into this folder. It will be copied to the storage space on the PC where it is located. In the same way, all the items in this folder remain accessible to all the computers on the network. It's a lot easier to exchange files than using a USB stick!

> Finally, you can make it easier for yourself to access this *Public* folder. Right-click on the *Users* folder containing the *Public folder*. In the pop-up menu, choose **Connect a network drive**.

> You can leave all the options as they are, or choose a network drive letter from the *Drive* menu if you wish. Click **Finish**.

> From now on, whenever this PC connects to the network, it will appear in *the This PC* list in Windows File Explorer.

SHARING A PARTICULAR FOLDER IN WINDOWS

The Public folder in Windows user accounts is specifically dedicated to file sharing. However, there's nothing to stop you sharing the folder of your choice.

> On one of the PCs connected to the network, for example, create a new folder on the desktop (right-click and choose **New > Folder**). Give this folder any name you like (we'll call it *SHARING* in our example).

> Right-click on the folder and choose **Grant access to > Specific people**.

> In the window that appears, click on the **downward-pointing arrow** next to the *Add* button, which is currently grey. Choose **Everyone** from the options.

> Click on the **Add** button that has become accessible, then on the **Share** button at the bottom of the window.

> Windows summarises your operation and shows the path to the newly shared folder. Click **Finish**.

> From another computer, access the PC on which you have just created and share your folder as explained above. This time the *Users* folder contains, in addition to the *Public* folder, a new folder with the user name of the remote PC;

> Open it. You have access to the *Desktop* folder. This is normal, as this is the *SHARING* folder was created. Open it to access it. Note that you will not be able to see the other items saved on the remote PC's Desktop: only the shared folder (and its contents) will remain visible and accessible;

> If you wish to stop sharing this particular folder, right-click on **its icon** again. From the context menu, choose **Grant access to > Remove access**.

XIV.3 INTERNET SERVICE: INSTANT MESSAGING AND VIDEOCONFERENCE (Skye, etc.)

XIV.3.1.INSTANT MESSAGING

Instant Messaging (IM) is a tool exchanging messages, often in writing, synchronously and in real time. IMs include a presence function, i.e. the ability to know whether a particular contact is present or available (a contact may appear to be present but not available, in a meeting for example) .[11]

EXAMPLE OF TOOLS THAT USE MESSAGING INSTANTANE

Facebook Messenger, Free, The instant messaging application from Facebook

Telegram

Free

An open-source messaging application

Viber

Free

A secure instant messaging application

Signal

Free

A secure, open source instant messaging application

[11] https://www.lemagit.fr, consulted on 20/10/2023 at 07H47'.

WhatsApp

Free
A benchmark in instant messaging

Microsoft Teams
Freemium
An enterprise collaboration platform belonging to the Office suite

XIV.3.2. VIDEOCONFERENCING

Teleconference in which the participants are linked by television circuits allowing the transmission of speech, moving images and graphic documents.

A videoconference is an **online meeting involving several participants, with incoming and outgoing audio and video streams**. You can see the expressions and reactions of the other participants, as well as hearing what they say.

We can also talk about videoconferencing. Generally speaking, **the two terms are completely synonymous**, and most people use one term rather than the other, depending on their preferences. At the moment, it's the more modern term "Visioconference" that wins out in France, in the sense that it seems more modern than a simple video.

Examples of videoconferencing software

1. Livestorm

3. Microsoft Teams
4. TeamViewer Meeting
5. Zoho Meeting
6. Zoom Meetings
7. Webex

XIV.4.FTP (File Transfer Protocol)

FTP stands for File Transfer Protocol. This communication protocol is used to exchange files between a server and a client. FTP is useful for transferring files between computers, either remotely or within a local network - your personal computer can even act as an FTP server. FTP can also be used to upload files from one computer to a web hosting account.

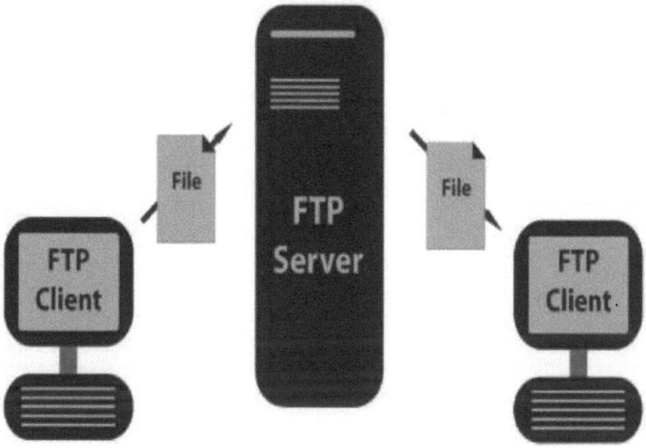

The protocol was first developed in 1971 by Abhay Bhushan Pandey, a student at the Massachusetts Institute of Technology. Since then, FTP has undergone several revisions to make it more secure. Today, there are at least three variants of the protocol - we'll talk about them in more detail in the following sections.

CHAPTER XV

WORD REVISION MENU

This tab allows you to check and review the document, as well as protect it.

1. **Verification** block :

- to check grammar and spelling: F7
- to search for text in reference works: Alt+left click
- to find synonyms: Shift+F7
- to set the language [note: when the Equation is used a lot, the system switches to English or Dutch...] ;
- to translate; note the difference between **Translation** and **Translation tooltip** [see tooltips opposite] ;

2. **Comments** block: to add comments [in a "tooltip" in the margin which is added], move from one to another or delete them;

3. block **Follow-up** :

- to highlight text changes in colour, either in the text or in tooltips;
- whether or not to display verification marks ;
- display the Verification pane ;

4. block **Modifications** :

- to accept or reject changes (which are then incorporated into the text or deleted) ;
- to go from one modification to another ;

5. **Compare** block :

- to compare two versions of the same document (in Revision mode) or combine the revisions of several authors in a single document;
- to display the source documents ;

6. **Protect** block: to protect against accidental modifications, by restricting formatting or modifications; you can set a password or not. You can protect the whole document, or just part of it.

CHAPTER XVI

EXCEL REVISION MENU

Under this tab, Excel offers you tools to check your document. Check spelling, look up a word in a dictionary, find a synonym or translate a word, protect the sheet, cell, workbook, share the workbook, track changes, etc.

XVI.1.SPELLING

To change the language when checking the spelling of a database or workbook, change the dictionary language during the spell checking process:

1. On the **Revision** tab in Excel or the **Home** tab in Access, click **Spelling.**
2. In the **Spelling** pane or dialog box, choose the desired language from the **Dictionary language** list.

XVI.2.SEARCH

Step 1: find the search function

Click on **Revision> Search**.

For Outlook, the Revision tab is only displayed in the message inspector. So you need to start a new message first.

Step 2: Find the search options

At the bottom of the Office Search pane, click **Search options**.

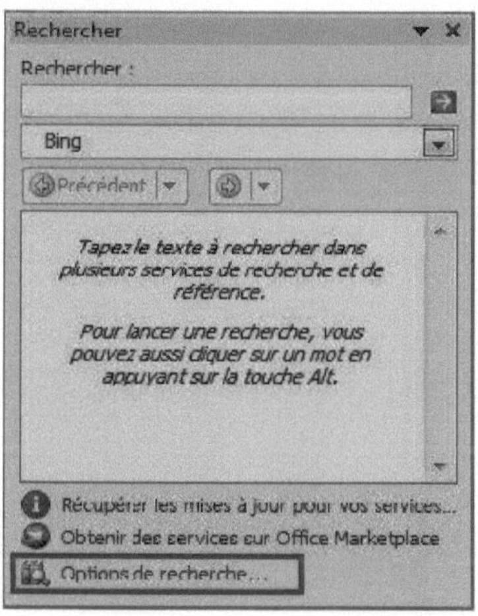

Another way of finding the search options is **to click on Options** > file > **Privacy Management Centre**. Then click on the Privacy Center **Settings** button to open the Privacy **Center** dialog box. Now click on the **Privacy Options** tab, then click on the **Search Options button**.

Step 3: Define your search options

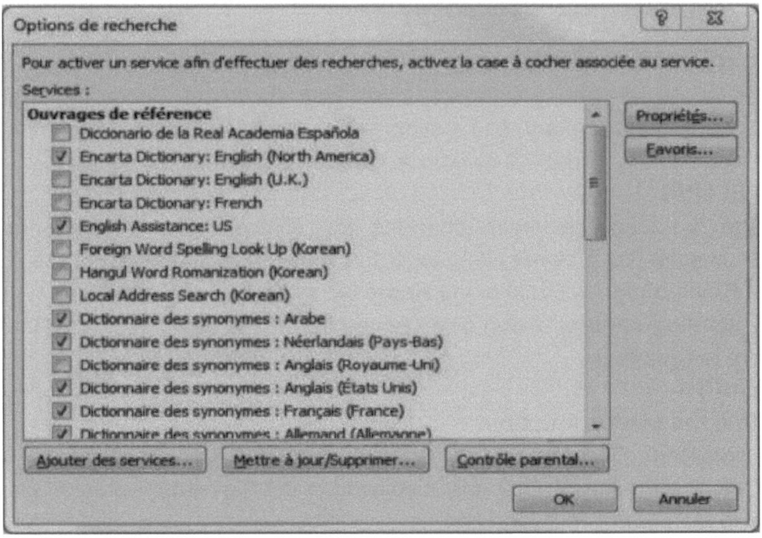

Perform at least one of the following operations:

- To enable or disable search services, tick or untick the boxes you want, then click **OK.**
- To add search services, click **Add services**, select or type the Internet address of the desired service in the **Address** box, then click **Add**. The service is automatically activated for searching, and appears in the **Search** list the next time you open the Office **Search** pane.

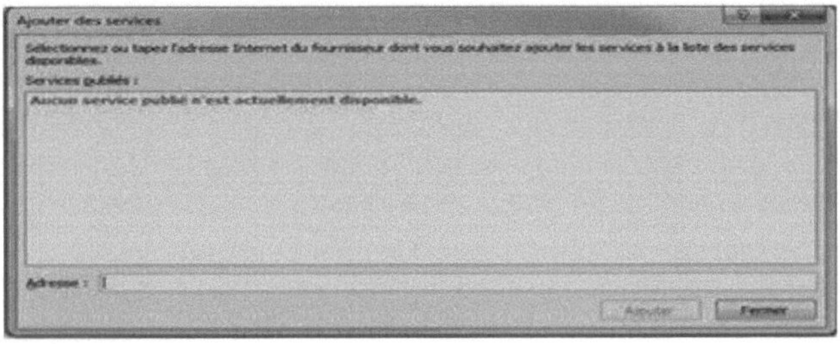

XVI.3.DICTIONARY OF SYNONYMS

Even in Excel, you may need to find synonyms for certain words.

1. Select a cell and enter the word **etonnant**.
2. Select the **Revision tab**.
3. Select the **Thesaurus** option.

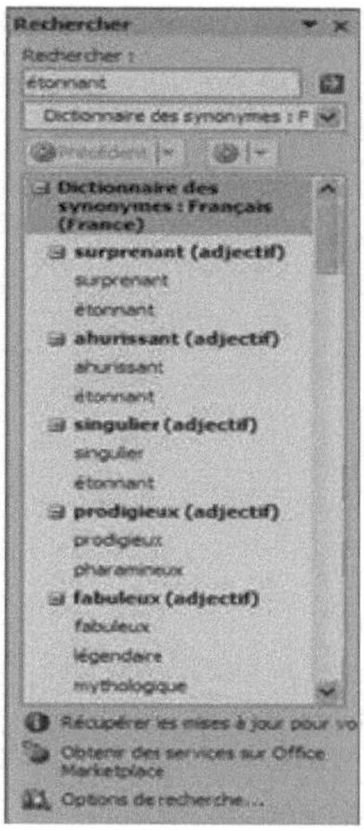

The synonym pane will open on the right-hand side of the screen with similar words. You can click on any word in the list to continue your search. You can also start searching for other words.

XVI.4.PROTECTING THE SHEET

Select the **Revision tab**. Press the **Protect sheet** button.

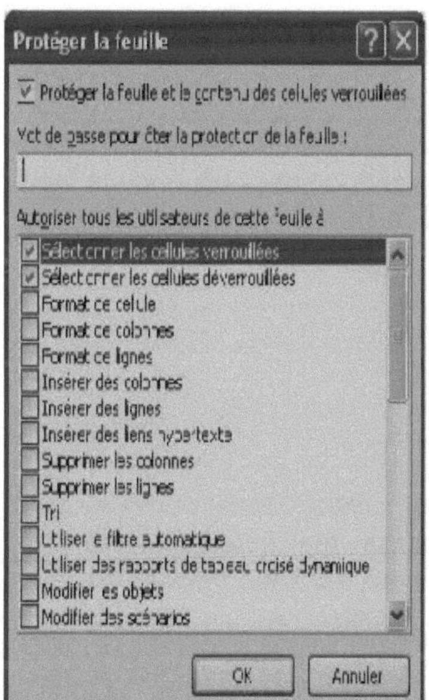

The window on the right will appear. You don't have to enter a password. It is

optional. You can leave this box empty and still protect your spreadsheet. There are several options that you can protect in addition to the content of the cells. The list includes all the elements over which you can have control in order to preserve the presentation or enable
certain options.

XVI.5.BINDER PROTECTION

You also have the option of protecting the entire workbook instead of just a single worksheet.

1. Select the **Revision tab**.
2. Press the **Protect folder** button.

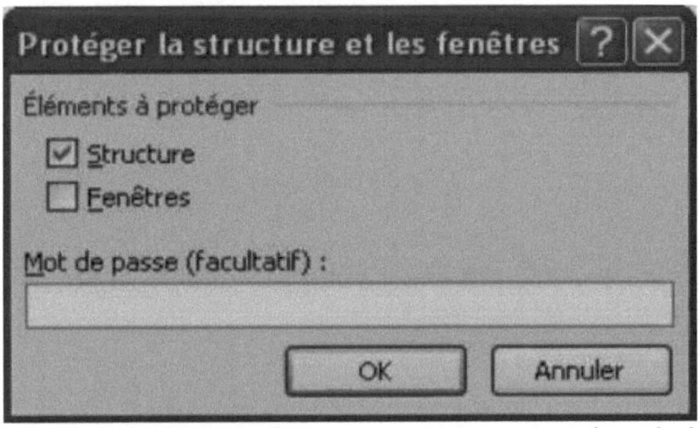

You can decide whether you want to protect the window structure or location if you have several documents or views open at the same time.

XVI.6.SHARING THE FOLDER

This option allows several users to enter or modify data at the same time in the same workbook. To ensure that important data is not overwritten by other users, the shared workbook will keep track of the changes made to each cell. You can review the modifications and decide which should be kept or changed.

Excel 2007 lets you share a workbook with several users. You need to save the workbook in a network folder that is accessible to other users. Then you must share the workbook. The owner of the document can withdraw the sharing of the workbook at any time. However, modifications not saved by users before sharing is stopped will not be retained.

XVI.7.MONITORING CHANGES

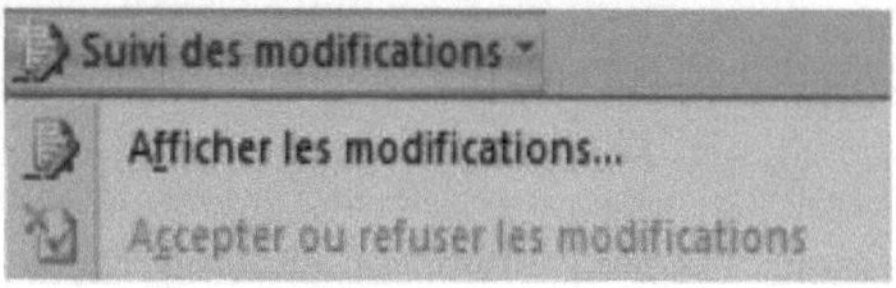

When sharing a document, you can ask to keep track of changes to cells. You can then decide on the content a cell if several people have entered different information in the same cell.

CHAPTER XVII

SAVE DATA

COMPUTING

A computer backup protects the data contained in your computer system by securing them, usually remotely from your own server .[10]

XVII.1.BURNING ON DVD/CD

Burning" is commonly referred to as copying music, images and videos from a PC to a blank CD or DVD. Conversely, "ripping" involves copying music, images and videos from a CD or DVD to a PC. Windows Media Player in Windows lets you do both.

Method 1: Using Windows 10's built-in burning function

- Insert a blank CD or DVD into the CD/DVD burner
- Open Windows **File Explorer**
- Select all the files you want to burn from their location
- Right-click then **Send** to and choose the CD to burn
- A **Burn a disc** window appears
- Enter a disk name
- Select **With a CD/DVD drive**, then click **Next** The files are now copied.

Your CD/DVD drive opens:

- Copy the files to the recorder drive
- Click on **Player Tools**
- Click on **Finish burning**

This is how Windows 10 burns your CD or DVD

Method 2: With Windows 10 Media Player

- Insert a blank CD or DVD
- Open **Windows Media Player**
- Click on **Burn** (top right)

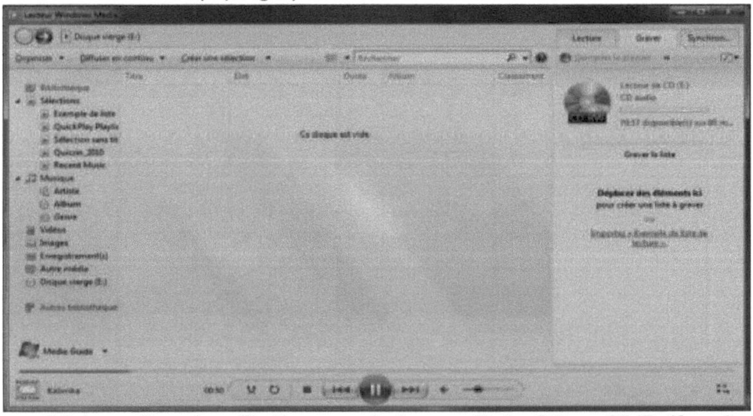

- Click on **Burning Options** and choose Data CD or DVD (for playback on

[10] https://www.appvizer.fr, consulted on 21/10/2023 at 07h03'

PCs and certain players that support these formats) or Audio CD (to burn MP3, WMA or WAV files for playback on all CD players and car radios).

- Open **Windows File Explorer** and navigate to the location of your files
- Make sure you can see both **File Explorer** and **Windows Media Player** at the same time
- Select your files and drag them to the **Windows Media Player** burn list
- Reorder your files if necessary
- Finally, click on **Start burning**

Windows will burn your CD or DVD and you will see a progress bar appear until the process is complete.

CHAPTER XVIII

FUNCTIONS (FINANCIAL, ACCOUNTING, LOGICAL)

XVIII.1.FINANCIAL FUNCTION

Here are the 5 most common Excel financial functions:

- **the NPM function** for calculating monthly payments ;
- **the VA function** to determine the amount of capital borrowed or invested ;
- **the VC function** to find out the amount to be paid at the end of a bank loan or the capital at the end of a life insurance policy;
- **the VPM function** to calculate the amount to be paid or invested each month;
- **the RATE function** to determine a percentage rate per period.

XVIII.2.ACCOUNTING FUNCTION

1. The VAN.PAYMENTS function

This function is used to determine the value of the company using the net present value of a series of discounted cash flows. Unlike the Excel NPV, the NPV.PAYMENTS function uses specific dates for the cash flows.

The syntax of the VAN.PAYMENTS function is as follows:

= VAN.PAYMENTS (Rates; Values; dates)

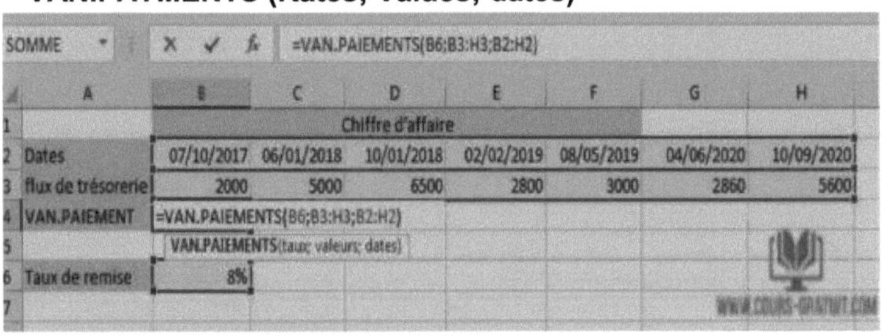

2. The SORT.PAYMENTS function

The TRI.PAYMENTS function is classified as an Excel financial function. It will calculate the internal rate of return (IRR) for a series of cash flows that may not be periodic. To do this, it assigns specific dates to each cash flow. The main advantage of Excel's IRR.PAYMENTS function is that it is possible to accurately model these planned cash flows in an unequal way.

The syntax of the function is as follows:

= TRI.PAYMENTS(cash flow; dates; [Estimate])

The estimate parameter is optional. It is your estimate of the internal rate of return. If the parameter is omitted, it takes on a constant value of 10%.

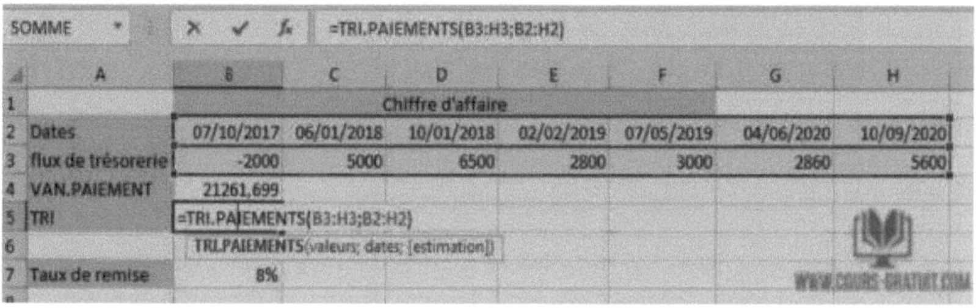

SOMME =TRI.PAIEMENTS(B3:H3;B2:H2)

	A	B	C	D	E	F	G	H
1		Chiffre d'affaire						
2	Dates	07/10/2017	06/01/2018	10/01/2018	02/02/2019	07/05/2019	04/06/2020	10/09/2020
3	flux de trésorerie	-2000	5000	6500	2800	3000	2860	5600
4	VAN.PAIEMENT	21261,699						
5	TRI	=TRI.PAIEMENTS(B3:H3;B2:H2)						
6		TRI.PAIEMENTS(valeurs; dates; [estimation])						
7	Taux de remise	8%						

Excel NPV and IRR assumes that the time periods in the cash flow are equal, but sometimes the cash flows are not evenly synchronised, so NPV.PAYMENTS and IRR.PAYMENTS are used to solve the problem.

3. The TRIM function

This function is very important for analysing the internal rate of return. It is a modified formula used when funds from one investment are used in another investment.

For example, if money for new land is invested in a new motor vehicle.

The syntax of the TRIM function is as follows:

=TRIM(cash flow; cost of borrowing; reinvestment rate)

Assuming that a company produces an internal rate of return, an IRR, with a financing rate of 6% and that the cash is reinvested in a vehicle at a rate of 5%, the MIRR will then be greater than the IRR.

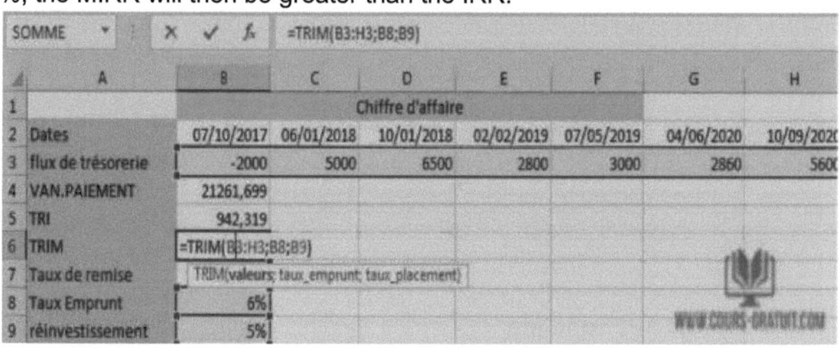

SOMME =TRIM(B3:H3;B8;B9)

	A	B	C	D	E	F	G	H
1		Chiffre d'affaire						
2	Dates	07/10/2017	06/01/2018	10/01/2018	02/02/2019	07/05/2019	04/06/2020	10/09/2020
3	flux de trésorerie	-2000	5000	6500	2800	3000	2860	5600
4	VAN.PAIEMENT	21261,699						
5	TRI	942,319						
6	TRIM	=TRIM(B3:H3;B8;B9)						
7	Taux de remise	TRIM(valeurs; taux_emprunt; taux_placement)						
8	Taux Emprunt	6%						
9	réinvestissement	5%						

4. The VPM function

The VPM function is used in real estate, commercial banking or in the financial analysis of positions with debt schedules. The formula is mainly used as a mortgage payment calculator. Once the interest is provided, the period and the mortgage available, you can easily calculate the payment amount.

The function syntax is as follows: **= VPM(rate; number of periods; current value)**

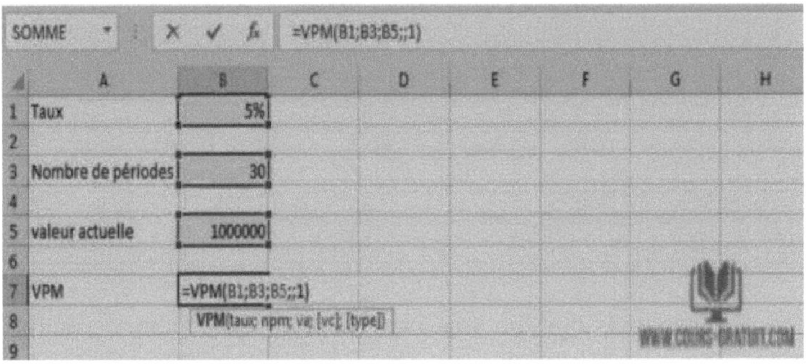

5. The INTPER function

INTPER calculates the interest rate for a fixed debt payment. The function works in conjunction with the VPM function. To obtain the capital payment for each period, you can separate the interest payments for each period and use the difference between VPM and INTPER.

The syntax of the INTPER function is :

= INTPER(rate; current period; total number of periods; current value)

Example: Calculation of interest payment in the fourth year over a 30-year loan repayment period with an interest rate of 5%.

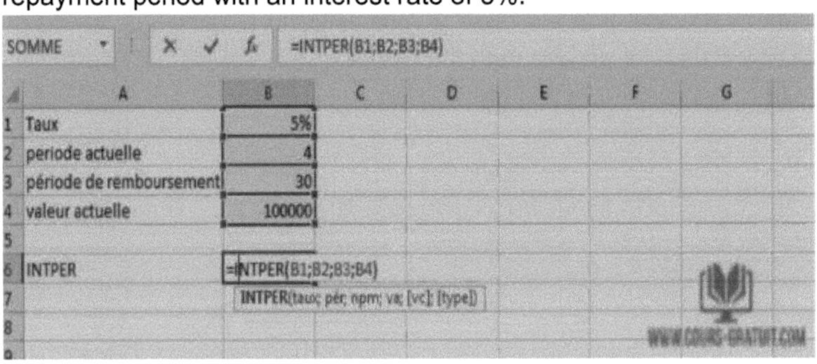

6. The RATE.STAFF function

This function is important in lending and borrowing businesses. It returns the annual interest rate for non-annual compounding.

The syntax of the function RATE.EFFECTIVE is: **= RATE.EFFECTIVE (interest rate; number of periods per year)**

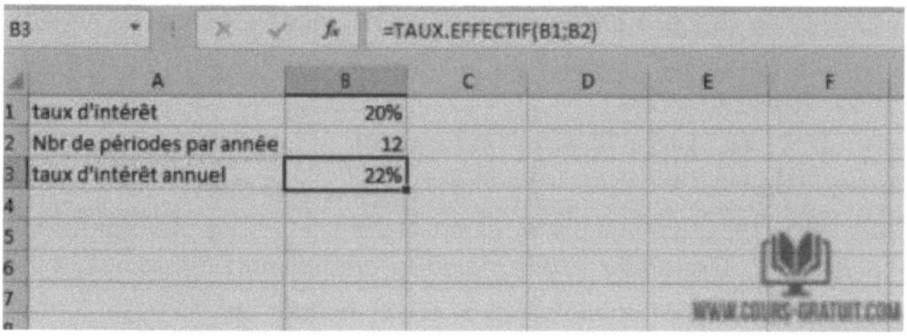

7. The VC function

This function helps you predict how much money you will have in the future, based on the starting amount, normal payments and compound interest rate.

The syntax of the VC function is as follows:

= VC (rate; number of periods; payments; start value; type)

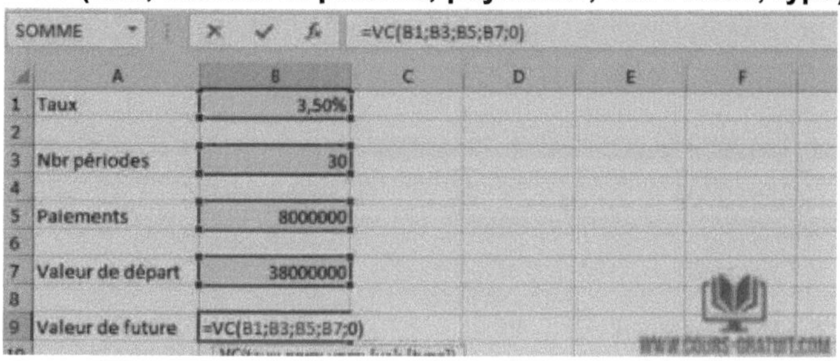

8. The DB function

This function is used by finance professionals to calculate depreciation. This allows them avoid creating a large declining balance.

The syntax of this function is: **= DB (cost ; recovery value ; lifetime / number of**
periods; current period)

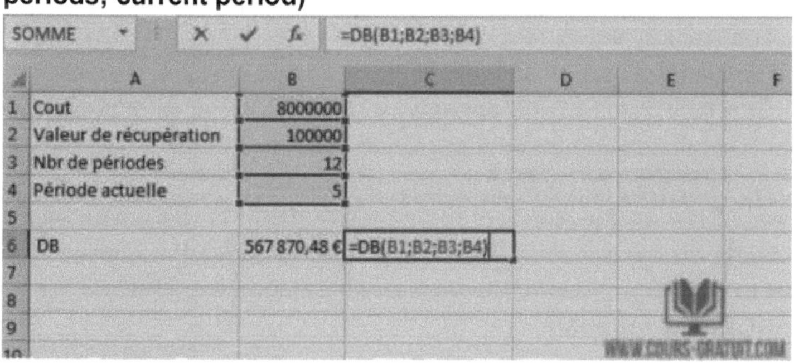

9. The RATE function

The Excel Rate function calculates the interest required to repay a specified amount of a loan or to reach a target amount on an investment, over a given period.

The syntax of the RATE function :

= RATE (npm ;vpm ; va ; [vc] ; [type] ; [estimate])

Npm: Mandatory. The total number of payment periods in a year.

Vpm : Compulsory. The payment made at each period cannot change during the life of the annuity. Generally, Vpm includes capital and interest, but no other charges or taxes. If Vpm is omitted, you must include the Vc argument.

Va: required. Present value - the total amount that a series of future payments is now worth.

Vc: Optional. The future value or cash balance you wish to achieve after the last payment. If Vc is omitted, it is assumed to be 0 (the future value of a loan, for example, is 0). If Vc is omitted, you must include the Vmp argument.

Type: Optional. The number 0 or 1 indicates when payments are due.

A11

	A	B	C	D	E	F
1	Nbr de périodes	10				
2	Coupon par période	100				
3	coût de la caution	-950				
4	valeur nominale de l'obligation	1000				
5	rendement à maturité	=TAUX(B1;B2;B3;B4;1)				
6	rendement à maturité	12%				
7						

10. The INTERET.ACC function

This function returns the accrued interest for a security that pays periodic interest.

The syntax of the function INTERET.ACC :

= INTERET.ACC (issue; prem_coupon; settlement; rate; nominal_value; frequency; [base]; [calculation_method]]

Issue: The date on which the security was issued.

Prem_coupon: The date on which the first interest will be paid.

Settlement : The security settlement date.

Rate: The annual coupon rate for security.

Face_Value: The face value of the security. If this parameter is omitted, the ACCRINT function will assume that the par value is set to $1,000.

Frequency: The frequency of security interest payments.

Base: Optional. This is the type of number of days to be used when calculating interest on the security. If this parameter is omitted, it implies that the base is set to 0.

11. The AMORDEGRC function:

Returns the depreciation for each accounting period using a depreciation factor.

The syntax is as follows:

= AMORDEGRC (cost; purchase date; first period; recovery; period; rate;

[base])

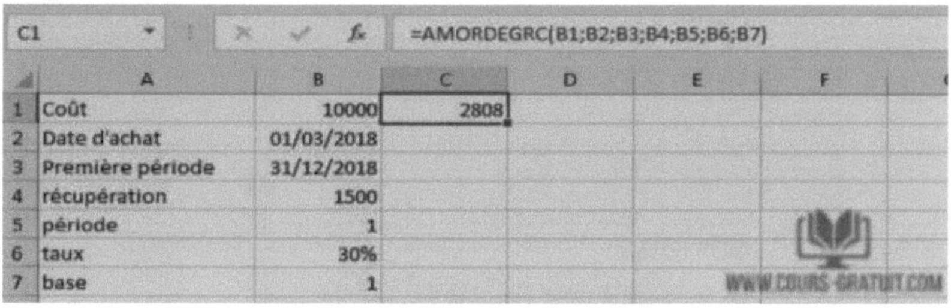

C1 | =AMORDEGRC(B1;B2;B3;B4;B5;B6;B7)

	A	B	C
1	Coût	10000	2808
2	Date d'achat	01/03/2018	
3	Première période	31/12/2018	
4	récupération	1500	
5	période	1	
6	taux	30%	
7	base	1	

12. The AMORLINC function :

Returns asset depreciation for each accounting period.

The syntax of the function is: **= AMORLINC (cost; purchase date; first period; recovery; period; rate; [base])**

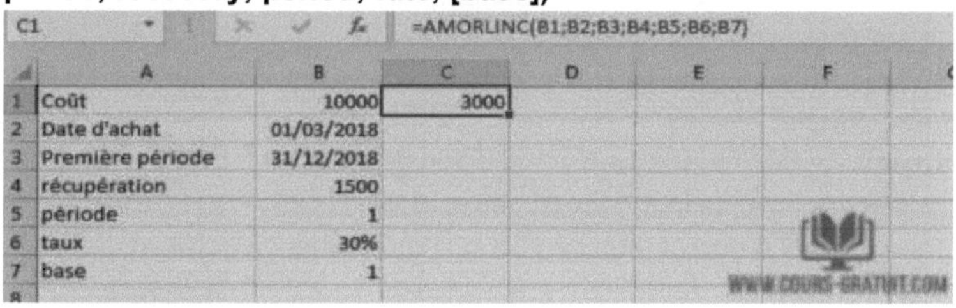

C1 | =AMORLINC(B1;B2;B3;B4;B5;B6;B7)

	A	B	C
1	Coût	10000	3000
2	Date d'achat	01/03/2018	
3	Première période	31/12/2018	
4	récupération	1500	
5	période	1	
6	taux	30%	
7	base	1	

13. The DDB function

This function returns the depreciation of an asset for a given period using the double decay method.

The syntax of the function is :

= DDB (cost; recovery; duration; period; [factor])

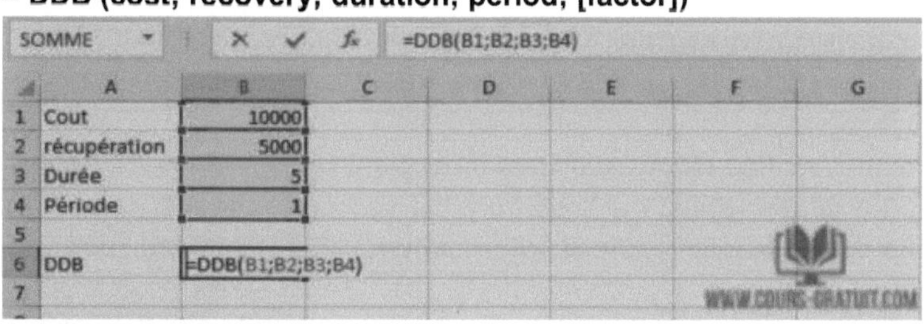

SOMME | =DDB(B1;B2;B3;B4)

	A	B
1	Cout	10000
2	récupération	5000
3	Durée	5
4	Période	1
5		
6	DDB	=DDB(B1;B2;B3;B4)
7		

14. The SYD function

Function SYD returns the depreciation of an asset for a given period in as a function of the sum of the years of the depreciation .

The syntax of the :

= SYD (cost; recovery; duration; period)

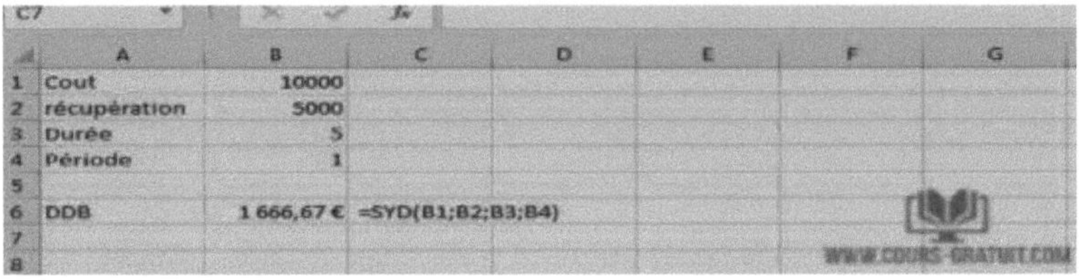

	A	B	C	D	E	F	G
1	Cout	10000					
2	récupération	5000					
3	Durée	5					
4	Période	1					
5							
6	DDB	1 666,67 €	=SYD(B1;B2;B3;B4)				
7							
8							

XVIII.3.LOGIC FUNCTIONS

Consider a set that respects several rules - AND

This "**AND**" function is used to check that several rules, conditions or criteria have been met. **Formula structure**: AND(*"condition 1"; "condition 2"*)**Example**: when the formula in the Excel cell is *=ET(A1>25;A1<100),* the value returned is True, False or #N/A depending on the value in cell A1.

Consider a set that respects at least one rule - OR

This "**OR**" function is used to ensure compliance with several selected rules, conditions and criteria.

Formula structure: OR("condition 1"; "condition 2")

Example: when the formula in the Excel cell is =OR(A1<25;A1>100), the value returned is True if one of the conditions is met, otherwise the value returned is False.

Test the conditions of a cell or value - SI / IF

This "**IF**" function is used to test the conditions of a cell or a value and return another value: If cell A1 is equal to cell B1, then the value is cell C1, otherwise the value is cell D1. **of the formula**: If(*"condition"; "then"; "otherwise'^*

Example: when the formula in the Excel cell is *=SI(A1=3;2;1),* if the value in cell A1 is "3" then the value returned is "2" otherwise the value returned is "1".

XVIII .4.SORTING ADVANCES

Advanced filters are also known as elaborate filters. We will therefore use both terms interchangeably.

Data table: the first line of an Excel data table must contain the names of the fields, also known as labels; the lines from the second to the last contain all the data (for example, information about customers): these lines are known as "records".

Each column contains, for each record, the data corresponding to the column label.

Record: line containing all the specific elements of a single, determined object (for example, the data for a customer, an item, etc.).

Label: each cell in the first row of the data table, naming the contents of the column (for example: "Last Name", "First Name", "Number", etc.).

A. Preliminary stage in the preparation of an advanced A filter

To use an elaborate filter, you need at least one data table and one criteria zone.

1. The data table must have column labels in the first row.
2. The criteria zone must have column labels in the first row and at least one row with one or more criteria, except for filtering duplicates (this subject will be covered in a later chapter).

Let's start with this table of data, which will enable us to test the filters we've developed without too much difficulty.

Let's expand this table down to row 5 and copy the row labels from this table to the 1st row of the Excel sheet.

	A	B	C	D	E	F	G
1	Prénom	Lieu	Naissance	Math	Français	Sciences	Moyenne
2							
3							
4							
5	Prénom	Lieu	Naissance	Math	Français	Sciences	Moyenne
6	Tanguy	Bruxelles	5/02/1998	8	6	8	7,3
7	Magali	Mons	11/11/1997	9	7	8	8,0
8	Isabelle	Liège	12/04/1997	6	7	5	6,0
9	Stéphane	Bruxelles	13/07/1997	7	9	8	8,0
10	Alain	Liège	3/12/1997	10	8	9	9,0
11	Philippe	Bruxelles	2/03/1998	8	8	7	7,7
12	Marie	Namur	30/06/1997	7	10	8	8,3

NB: the labels in the criteria area must have the same spelling as the labels in the data table.

B. How to activate the elabore A filter

- Excel 2003 Menu [Data] - Filter - Advanced filter.
- Excel 2007 and later : **Data**] tab, Sort and filter group, **Advance** command.

The dialog box then appears, with the Ranges field filled in if the cursor is in one of the cells in the data table.

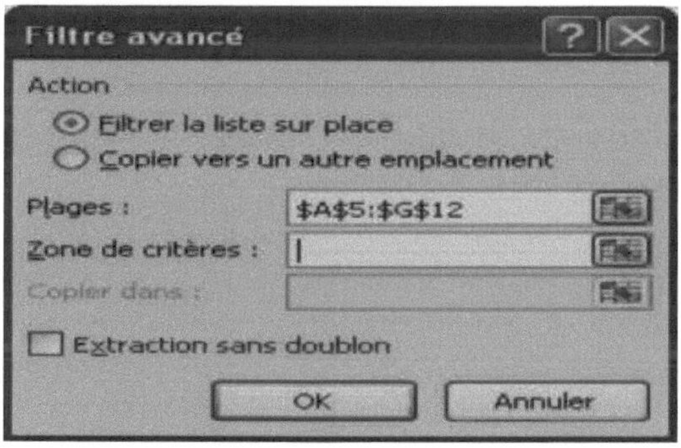

C. A few simple examples.

C.1 First example A

Let's start with a simple example: filtering rows (records) where the column **Location** is equal to "Brussels".

In cell **B2**, just below the **Location** label, we enter the value "Brussels".

In the Sort and filter group on the **[Data]** tab, click on the **Advance** command. **The Advanced Filter** dialog box appears.

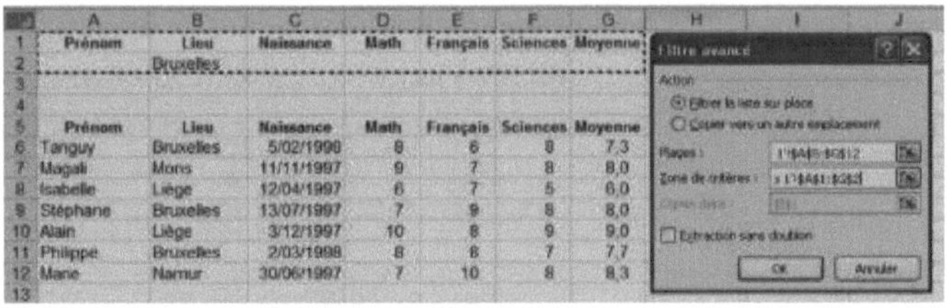

Let's analyse each option in this box.

- **Filter the list on the spot**: filter directly in the Excel cell area where the start data is placed and which is declared by the **Ranges** option (in our example **A5:G12**).
- **Copy to another location**: used to create the filter list in another location defined by the **Copy to** option.
- **Ranges**: the area to be filtered.
- **Criteria area**: indicates the range of cells where we have inserted our filter criteria (in our example **A2:G2**).
- **Copy to**: designates the cell or range of cells from which the filtered rows will be copied. This option is only available if **Copy to another location** is ticked.
- **Extraction without duplicates**: avoids displaying duplicate data either with the filter in place or by copying to another location.

We therefore opt for the in-place filter, taking the range as **A5:G12** and the criterion area as **A1:G2**. Confirm with **OK** and see the result.

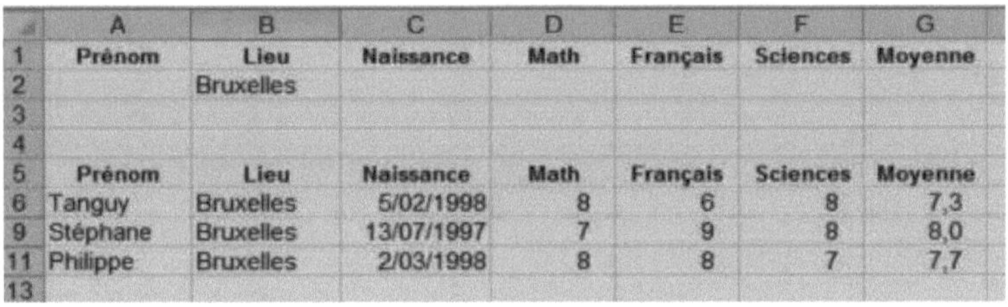

	A	B	C	D	E	F	G
1	Prénom	Lieu	Naissance	Math	Français	Sciences	Moyenne
2		Bruxelles					
3							
4							
5	Prénom	Lieu	Naissance	Math	Français	Sciences	Moyenne
6	Tanguy	Bruxelles	5/02/1998	8	6	8	7,3
9	Stéphane	Bruxelles	13/07/1997	7	9	8	8,0
11	Philippe	Bruxelles	2/03/1998	8	8	7	7,7
13							

We can see that the numbers in the filtered lines are blue and that lines 7, 8, 10 and 12 are hidden: this is because the value in these lines is different from the criterion chosen ("Brussels").

This result could, of course, have been obtained using a simple filter.

To display the data again, simply click on the **Clear** command, which is in the same group as the **Elaborate filter** command.

C.2 Second example A

Let's now filter the records for which the location is "Brussels" AND whose date of birth is greater than or equal to 1st January 2008.

Add the value >=01/01/2008 to cell **C2**. Then execute the same order with the same options.

	A	B	C	D	E	F	G
1	Prénom	Lieu	Naissance	Math	Français	Sciences	Moyenne
2		Bruxelles	>=01/01/1998				
3							
4							
5	Prénom	Lieu	Naissance	Math	Français	Sciences	Moyenne
6	Tanguy	Bruxelles	5/02/1998	8	6	8	7,3
11	Philippe	Bruxelles	2/03/1998	8	8	7	7,7

We can see that there are now only two recordings that meet these two combined criteria.

C.3 Third example A

Then apply a filter by adding a criterion:(Location=Brussels and Date of birth>=01/01/1998) **OR** (Average>7.5).

To obtain the discounted result, add the value **>7.5** in **G3** (**Average** column**).**

In the dialogue box, change the criteria zone to **A1:G3**.

	A	B	C	D	E	F	G
1	Prénom	Lieu	Naissance	Math	Français	Sciences	Moyenne
2		Bruxelles	>=01/01/1998				
3							>7,5
4							
5	Prénom	Lieu	Naissance	Math	Français	Sciences	Moyenne
6	Tanguy	Bruxelles	5/02/1998	8	6	8	7,3
7	Magali	Mons	11/11/1997	9	7	8	8,0
9	Stéphane	Bruxelles	13/07/1997	7	9	8	8,0
10	Alain	Liège	3/12/1997	10	8	9	9,0
11	Philippe	Bruxelles	2/03/1998	8	8	7	7,7
12	Marie	Namur	30/06/1997	7	10	8	8,3

In conclusion, we can see that placing criteria on the same line is equivalent to the **AND** function; however, if we use several lines, it is equivalent to the **OR** function.

C.4 Fourth example A

This example is practically the same as the previous one, except that in the second line (**OR**) we add Brussels to the **Location** criterion.

This means that we filter the records using :

(Place=Brussels) AND (Birth>=01/01/1998 OR Average>7.5), which can also be written as (Place=Brussels AND Date of birth>=01/01/1998) OR (Place=Brussels AND Average>7.5).

	A	B	C	D	E	F	G
1	Prénom	Lieu	Naissance	Math	Français	Sciences	Moyenne
2		Bruxelles	>=01/01/1998				
3		Bruxelles					>7,5
4							
5	Prénom	Lieu	Naissance	Math	Français	Sciences	Moyenne
6	Tanguy	Bruxelles	5/02/1998	8	6	8	7,3
9	Stéphane	Bruxelles	13/07/1997	7	9	8	8,0
11	Philippe	Bruxelles	2/03/1998	8	8	7	7,7

D. The filter is based on several criteria A

In the previous examples, we used a single filter criterion per column; in the following examples, we will use several criteria simultaneously.

For example, we want to filter the data of people whose average ratings are between 7.5 and 9.

Important clarification: until now, we had the same number of columns in the criteria area as in the data table. This is absolutely unnecessary, as only the columns and their labels relevant to the criteria need be present.

We will therefore use two columns of criteria with the same **Average** label, as shown in the example below.

In the dialog box, the Criteria zone option will therefore refer to cells **A1:B2**.

	A	B	C	D	E	F	G
1	Moyenne	Moyenne					
2	>=7,5	<=9					
3							
4							
5	Prénom	Lieu	Naissance	Math	Français	Sciences	Moyenne
7	Magali	Mons	11/11/1997	9	7	8	8,0
9	Stéphane	Bruxelles	13/07/1997	7	9	8	8,0
10	Alain	Liège	3/12/1997	10	8	9	9,0
11	Philippe	Bruxelles	2/03/1998	8	8	7	7,7
12	Marie	Namur	30/06/1997	7	10	8	8,3

If we wish to apply an additional criterion, for example, people from Brussels with an average between 7 and 9, we will add a criteria column and in the dialog box, the Criteria zone option will therefore refer to cells **A1:C2**, as shown in the example below.

	A	B	C	D	E	F	G
1	Moyenne	Moyenne	Lieu				
2	>=7,5	<=9	Bruxelles				
3							
4							
5	Prénom	Lieu	Naissance	Math	Français	Sciences	Moyenne
9	Stéphane	Bruxelles	13/07/1997	7	9	8	8,0
11	Philippe	Bruxelles	2/03/1998	8	8	7	7,7

E. The calculated criteriaA

E.1. Examples of calculated criteriaA

One of the great advantages of the elaborate filter, which is not well known, is use of calculated criteria.

To use them, enter a formula instead of a constant and place a name as the column label that is not found as a header in the data table.

So, if we want to filter the data for people born in 1997, we'll place a column with the label **YearName** and in the next row the formula **=YEAR(C6)=1997**.

A2 — =ANNEE(C6)=1997

	A	B	C	D	E	F	G
1	AnneeNaiss						
2	FAUX						
3							
4							
5	Prénom	Lieu	Naissance	Math	Français	Sciences	Moyenne
6	Tanguy	Bruxelles	5/02/1998	8	6	8	7,3
7	Magali	Mons	11/11/1997	9	7	8	8,0
8	Isabelle	Liège	12/04/1997	6	7	5	6,0

We see that cell **A2**, which contains the formula **=YEAR(C6)=1997** and refers to cell **C6**, returns **FALSE**: the value of the cell in **C6** is 5 February 1998, so the year is 1998.

A2 =ANNEE(C6)=1997

	A	B	C	D	E	F	G
1	Année						
2	FAUX						
3							
4							
5	Prénom	Lieu	Naissance	Math	Français	Sciences	Moyenne
7	Magali	Mons	11/11/1997	9	7	8	8,0
8	Isabelle	Liège	12/04/1997	6	7	5	6,0
9	Stéphane	Bruxelles	13/07/1997	7	9	8	8,0
10	Alain	Liège	3/12/1997	10	8	9	9,0
12	Marie	Namur	30/06/1997	7	10	8	8,3

In conclusion: when we use criteria calculated in filters elaborated: the column label must have a different name to that a label in the data table; the criterion must be a formula or a series of nested formulas which must return **TRUE** or **FALSE ;**

The logical test MUST be performed on one or more cells in the first row of the data table.

We could, of course, add calculated criteria.

For example, let's filter out the records of people born in 1997 whose maths score is equal to or higher than the average points obtained in maths.

Add a criterion column with the label **MoyMath** and the formula **=D6>MOYENNE($D$6:$D$12)**. Knowing that the average obtained in maths for all the people registered is **7.8**, the final result is two filter records.

	A	B	C	D	E	F	G
1	AnneeNaiss	MoyMath					
2	FAUX	VRAI					
3							
4							
5	Prénom	Lieu	Naissance	Math	Français	Sciences	Moyenne
7	Magali	Mons	11/11/1997	9	7	8	8,0
10	Alain	Liège	3/12/1997	10	8	9	9,0

In this case, of course, we could have limited ourselves to a single column containing the calculated criterion with, for example, the label **AnSupMoy** and the formula :

=**AND(YEAR(C6)=1997;D6>=MEAN($D$6:$D$12))**

or even

=(ANNEE(C6)=1997)*(D6>=MOYENNE($D$6:$D$12)).

CHAPTER XIX

EXCELLENT FILTERS

A filter is an Excel function that allows you to display only certain data in your table, according to one or more criteria.

XIX.1.AUTOMATIC FILTER

It is important to use the Automatic Filter function to search for, display or hide values in one or more columns of data. You can filter according to the choices available in a list, or search for the data you are looking for. When you filter data, entire rows are hidden if the values in one or more columns do not meet the filter criteria.

To apply an automatic filter, follow these steps :

1. Select the data to be filtered.
2. Click on **Data> Filter**.
3. Click on the H arrow in the column header and decide whether you want to select specific values or perform a search.

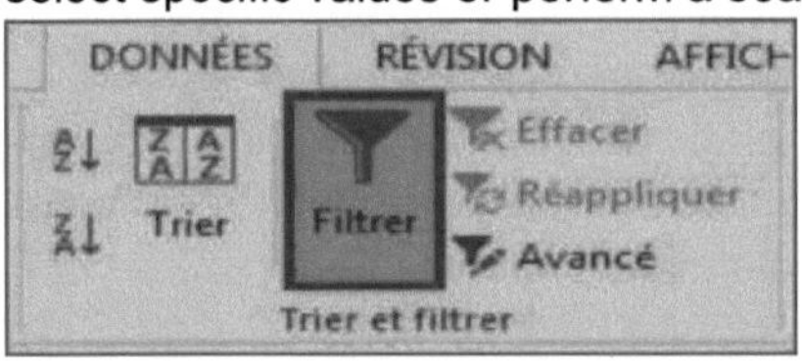

4. **Choose specific values: Uncheck (Select all)** to uncheck all the boxes, then check the boxes for the specific values you want to see.

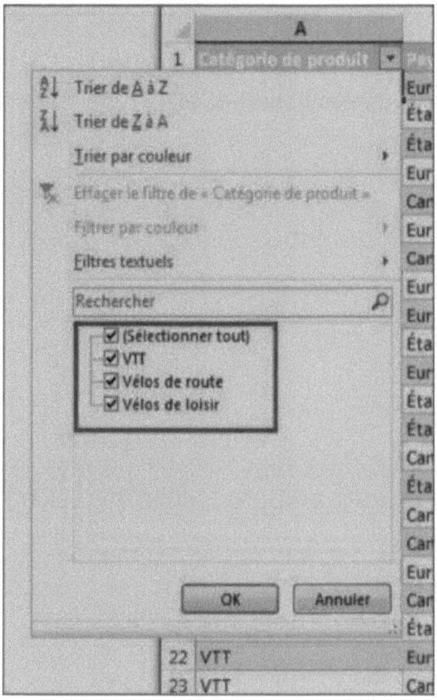

5. **Search for values:** In the search box, type the text or numbers you are looking for.

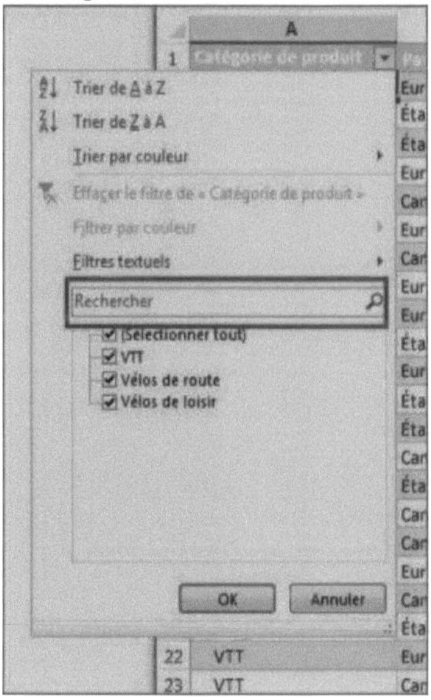

6. Click **OK** to apply the filter.

XIX.2.TEXT FILTERS

For example, in our table below, all you need to do to find out what equipment

is affected for the financial and production sectors is click on the database and click on "filter".
On each column appear Arrows which are drop-down lists that allow you to use all the possibilities notified on the
left of the image.

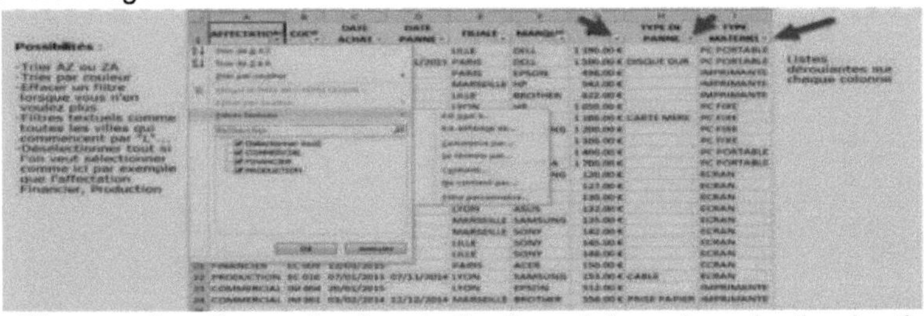

Let's filter on allocation and ask only for financials and production by ticking these two boxes.

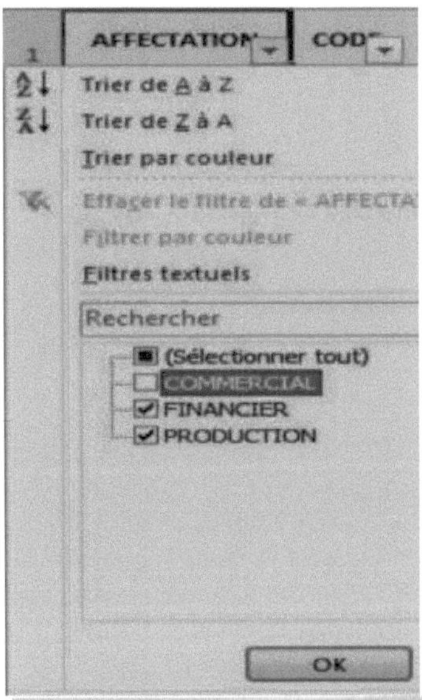

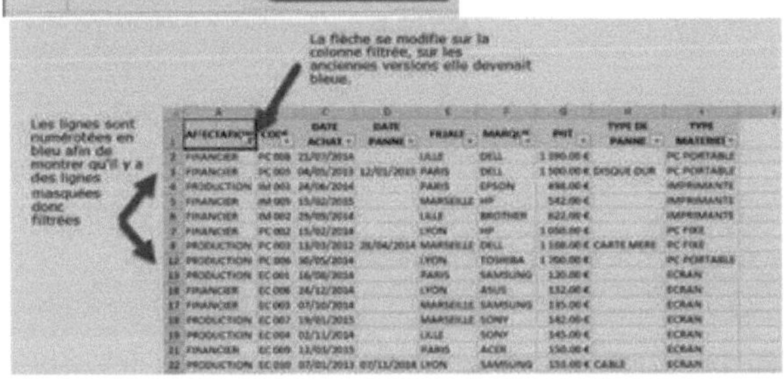

You can combine several filters to complete your analysis. For example, based on this result, I only want the cities of Lille and Paris.

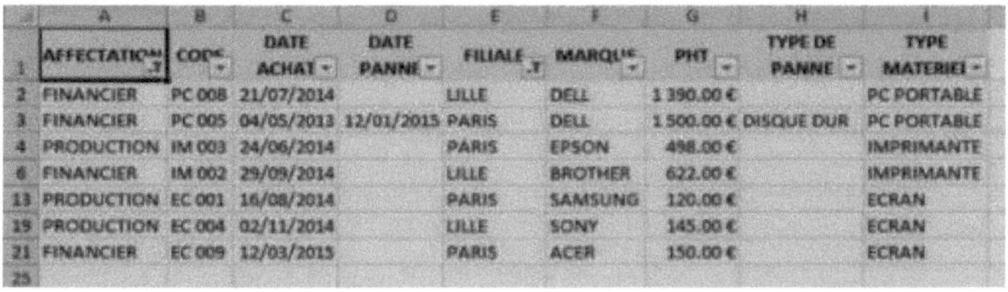

	A	B	C	D	E	F	G	H	I
1	AFFECTATION	CODE	DATE ACHAT	DATE PANNE	FILIALE	MARQUE	PHT	TYPE DE PANNE	TYPE MATERIEL
2	FINANCIER	PC 008	21/07/2014		LILLE	DELL	1 390.00 €		PC PORTABLE
3	FINANCIER	PC 005	04/05/2013	12/01/2015	PARIS	DELL	1 500.00 €	DISQUE DUR	PC PORTABLE
4	PRODUCTION	IM 003	24/06/2014		PARIS	EPSON	498.00 €		IMPRIMANTE
6	FINANCIER	IM 002	29/09/2014		LILLE	BROTHER	622.00 €		IMPRIMANTE
13	PRODUCTION	EC 001	16/08/2014		PARIS	SAMSUNG	120.00 €		ECRAN
19	PRODUCTION	EC 004	02/11/2014		LILLE	SONY	145.00 €		ECRAN
21	FINANCIER	EC 009	12/03/2015		PARIS	ACER	150.00 €		ECRAN
25									

So let's continue from this result and I only want the screens.
I only have 3 results left.

	A	B	C	D	E	F	G	H	I
1	AFFECTATION	CODE	DATE ACHAT	DATE PANNE	FILIALE	MARQUE	PHT	TYPE DE PANNE	TYPE MATERIEL
13	PRODUCTION	EC 001	16/08/2014		PARIS	SAMSUNG	120.00 €		ECRAN
19	PRODUCTION	EC 004	02/11/2014		LILLE	SONY	145.00 €		ECRAN
21	FINANCIER	EC 009	12/03/2015		PARIS	ACER	150.00 €		ECRAN
25									

The number recordings displayed by the filter is shown at the bottom.
on your Excel sheet.

Imagine this on a database not of 23 records like this one but of more than 5000 rows, and the time saved.

And don't forget, once your filters have been run, you can SORT by Subsidiary, for example. Better still, you can COPY the resulting filter on a new sheet if you want to use it further.

XIX.3.DATE FILTERS

1. Click on a single cell in a dataset.
2. On the Data tab, in the Sort and filter group, click Filter.

The arrows in the column headings appear.

	A	B	C	D	E
1	Last Nan	Sales	Count	Date	
2	Smith	$16,753.00	UK	4/25/2013	
3	Johnson	$14,808.00	USA	1/5/2016	
4	Williams	$10,644.00	UK	4/13/2015	
5	Jones	$1,390.00	USA	9/5/2016	
6	Brown	$4,865.00	USA	1/21/2013	
7	Williams	$12,438.00	UK	4/6/2013	
8	Johnson	$9,339.00	UK	11/14/2016	
9	Smith	$18,919.00	USA	7/16/2014	
10	Jones	$9,213.00	USA	1/26/2015	
11	Jones	$7,433.00	UK	11/1/2013	
12	Brown	$3,255.00	USA	5/18/2015	
13	Williams	$14,867.00	USA	1/5/2015	
14	Williams	$19,302.00	UK	8/23/2016	
15	Smith	$9,698.00	USA	1/17/2016	
16					

3. Click on the arrow next to Date.
4. Click on Select all to clear all the checkboxes, click on the + sign next to 2015, then on the checkbox next to January.

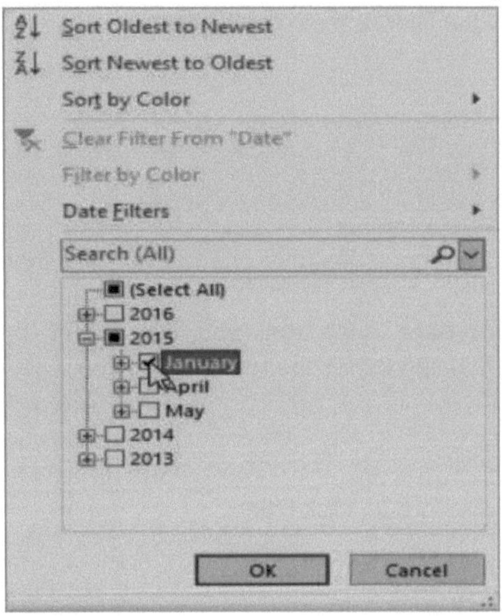

5. Click on OK.

Result. **Exceller** only displays sales in 2015, in January.

	A	B	C	D	E
1	Last Nan	Sales	Count	Date	
10	Jones	$9,213.00	USA	1/26/2015	
13	Williams	$14,867.00	USA	1/5/2015	
16					

6. Click on the arrow next to Date.

7. Click on Select all to tick all the boxes.
8. Click Date Filters (this option is available because the Date column contains dates) and select Last Month from the list.

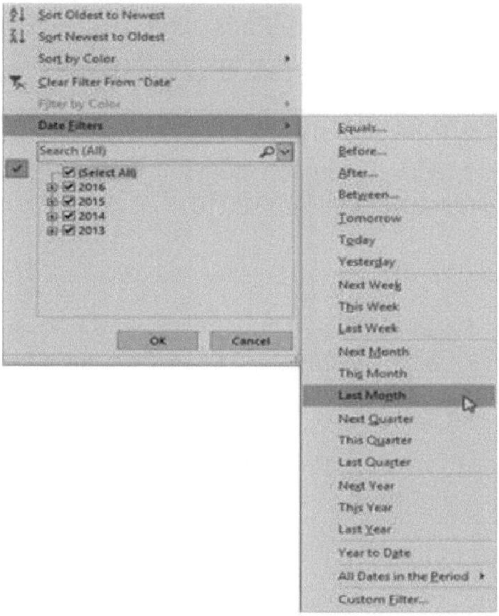

Result: Excel only displays last month's sales.

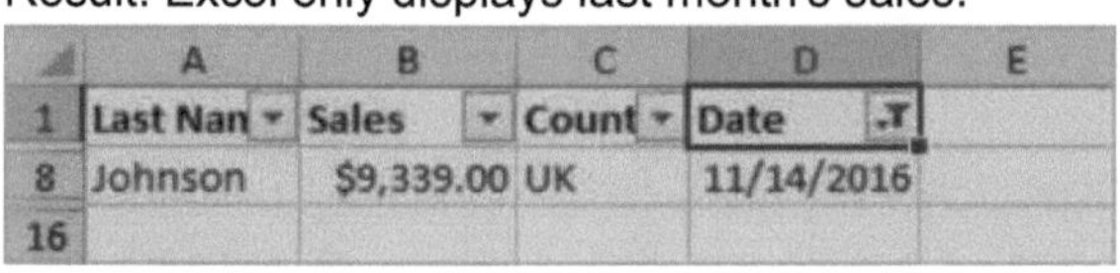

Note: this and many other date filters depend on the current date.

BIBLIOGRAPHY

❖ **The works**

- Curriculum National des Humanites Techniques Commercials, 2016 ;
- Doug Lowe, *Les Reseaux pour les nuls*, 10e edition, Paris, First, 2017 ;
- Jacques LONCHAMP, introduction aux systemes informatique, Paris, Dunod, 201 ;
- G. PUJOLLE, *Initiation aux reseaux,* Paris, Eyrolles, 2001 ;
- Guillaume PLOUIN, *Cloud computing. Securite, gouvernance du SI hybride et panorama du marché,* 4e edition, Dunod, Paris, 2016.

❖ **Websites:**

- https://actualiteinformatique.fr
- https://www.lemagit.fr
- www.location-entretien-photocopieur.fr
- www.appvizer.fr
- https://support.microsoft.com
- www.techno-science.net
-

MIX
Papier aus verantwortungsvollen Quellen
Paper from responsible sources
FSC® C105338

Printed by Books on Demand GmbH, Norderstedt / Germany